12 SIMPLE SECRETS

TO EXPERIENCING JOY

in everyday relationships

12 SIMPLE SECRETS

TO EXPERIENCING JOY

in everyday relationships

GLENN VAN EKEREN

HigherLife
DEVELOPMENT SERVICES
Orlando, Florida

12 Simple Secrets to Experiencing Joy in Everyday Relationships by Glenn Van Ekeren

Copyright © 2009 Glenn Van Ekeren
All rights reserved

Published by HigherLife Development Services, Inc.
2342 Westminster Terrace
Oviedo, Florida 32765
(407) 563-4806
www.ahigherlife.com

Cover Design: DaNita Naimoli

ISBN 13: 978-0-9793227-6-1
ISBN 10: 0-9793227-6-6

Scripture quotations marked KJV are from the *King James Version* of the Bible.

Scripture quotations marked NAS are from the *New American Standard Bible.* Copyright © 1960, 1962, 1963, 1968, 1971, 1972, 1973, 1975, 1977 by the Lockman Foundation. Used by permission.

Scripture quotations marked NIV are from the *Holy Bible, New International Version.* Copyright © 1973, 1978, 1984, International Bible Society. Used by permission.

09 10 11 12 13 — 8 7 6 5 4 3 2 1

Printed in the United States of America

CONTENTS

Section Three: Forgiveness

Section Four: Kindness

Section Five: Friendship

Section Six: Encouragement

Section Seven: Understanding

Section Eight: Communication

Section Nine: Gratitude

Section Ten: Generosity

Section Eleven: Empathy

Section Twelve: Hope

ACKNOWLEDGMENTS

My heartfelt thanks to the following people:

My wife, Marty, for her continual encouragement, friendship, and willingness to stick with me through thick and thin.

To my children, Matt and Katy, for believing in their dad and allowing me to tell stories about them.

To all my friends and family who encouraged me to turn my writing dreams into reality.

INTRODUCTION

RELATIONSHIPS ARE AS OLD AS creation. They are the driving force behind most everything we do in life. They influence our moods, our feelings, our hopes, and our dreams. They are part of our past, present, and future. They help us to stop thinking only of ourselves and help us to learn more about ourselves as we live life in this large world.

The older I get, the more I'm convinced of the direct correlation between our success with relationships and virtually everything of significance in life. When relationships are successful, life is good. When they fail, along with them go health, fulfillment, and the joy of living.

Wherever we go, whatever we do, whatever careers we have chosen, whatever activities we are involved in, whatever good or bad news reports we hear, whatever financial crises, wars, or storms that happen, there is a common denominator in every area of life: people. We can't live without them, but let's be honest: sometimes it's very tough to live with them.

Relationships can be a source of wonderful fulfillment, satisfaction, and joy in life. They can also be a major pain in the...*uh*, neck. There is an ongoing pull between what we want our relationships to be and what they are. *Twelve Simple Secrets to Experiencing Joy in Everyday Relationships* is about the simple, yet often forgotten, accumulation of little things that contribute to building our relationships into what we want them to become.

So many books, manuals, and seminars have been written about relationships. So many poems, songs, and letters are inspired by them. So many cards, so many commercials, so many movies deal with relationships. So, why this book? It might seem like the topic has been exhausted.

Considering all the advice we've received, it should be easy to sustain harmonious, cooperative, and mutually beneficial relationships. In reality, we aren't there. Maybe we read but don't respond; maybe we listen but don't understand. Maybe we know what to do but fail to take action. Whatever the case, relationships are going one way or the other. They are either getting better and growing, or they're slipping and sliding downhill.

The ability or inability to cultivate quality relationships is a choice. When we choose to live for ourselves, relationships suffer. Choosing to focus attention and invest energies in your spouse, children, friends, neighbors, and coworkers will reap positive returns. Successful relationships are a natural outgrowth of this principle: the way we treat others affects the way they treat us. The tricky part? To not allow the way another person treats us to determine the way we treat them.

Think about this. What comes to the mind of a person when he or she sees you? Positive thoughts? Does a sense of encouragement come with you? Or, have you developed habits that have turned you into a "thorn" in someone's life?

I hope that when people see me coming, their first thought is not, "There goes the thorn in my life." I strive each day to be a positive influence in people's lives, to become what I often call a "picker-upper person." Picker-upper people are masters at building and maintaining quality relationships. They understand the dynamics for improving their casual and most intimate interactions. To them, love is a verb. Genuinely caring for others is a way of life.

Picker-upper people transform lives and relationships by activating the qualities of people-building.

This book is all about making a positive difference in people's lives. And I confess—I probably wrote it for myself as much as anyone else. This book contains the relationship principles I teach to audiences, preach to my children, and struggle to activate in my daily encounters. As I wrote, new ideas continually surfaced on ways I could improve my effectiveness with people. This book is packed with timeless wisdom, proven principles, simple actions, and contemporary insight that will help you experience increased enjoyment in your relationships.

So, get ready. You can become a picker-upper person. Choose any section in this book, and you will discover a variety of insightful comments, entertaining illustrations, and practical strategies that will help you:

- Accept people for who they are
- Identify what people need to feel good about themselves
- Make your relationships bloom
- Get along with difficult people
- Effectively deal with conflict
- Develop a sincere interest in others
- Build on people's positive qualities
- Forgive hurtful actions
- Encourage, uplift, and motivate others to reach their potential
- Become the type of person people enjoy being around

I assume that you're reading this book because you want more out of your relationships. If you want success, great! If you're looking for strategies to get your own way, sorry. If you want people to enjoy being with you, help is here. If you want a scheme to manipulate others, don't bother reading any further. If you're willing to commit yourself to the people in your life, your journey through this book will be delightful and beneficial.

Renew your desire. Increase your awareness. Learn new skills to become a life-long picker-upper person. This down-to-earth book is flowing with how-to's for making relationships work. So, enter in, and welcome joy into all of your relationships.

Section One

LOVE

Chapter 1

GOOD ADVICE—
WRONG APPLICATION

There is little doubt that most of us long for stronger, more creative and rewarding ways of loving each other.

—Leo F. Buscaglia[1]

CONSTANT CONFLICT CAUSED AN ENGAGED couple to question their wedding plans. The man, concerned he could lose the woman he loved, realized he had no idea how to handle many unresolved issues. So, he sought the advice of a counselor who suggested the problems could be solved if he would take up biking. "I want you to ride ten miles a day for the next two weeks and then check back with me."

Two weeks later the man reported back to his counselor as requested. "So, how are you and your fiancée doing now?" the counselor inquired.

"How should I know," the man replied, "I'm one hundred forty miles away from home, and I haven't talked to her for fourteen days."

There will always be challenges and problems in relationships. No problem! Dr. Theodore Rubin advises in *One to One*: "The problem is not that there are problems. The problem is expecting otherwise and thinking that having problems is a problem."[2]

Abundant advice is available from assorted sources for anyone wishing to enrich their relationships. Unfortunately, none of that advice works unless you're willing to step up your investment in people.

If you remember the following, your relationships will never be the same.

1. Creating and nourishing relationships is hard work.
2. There will always be problems.
3. Relationships are worth every ounce of effort it takes to work through the unavoidable challenges.

This is good advice, if I must say so myself. Apply it *now*.

> I like long walks, especially when they are taken by people who annoy me.
>
> —Fred Allen[3]

Chapter 2

THE FLIP SIDE OF LOVE

Love has nothing to do with what you are expecting to get—
only what you are expecting to give—which is everything.
— Katherine Hepburn[1]

W HAT YOU WILL RECEIVE IN return varies, but it really has no connection with what you give. You give because you love and cannot help giving. If you are very lucky, you may be loved back. That is delicious, but it does not necessarily happen.

I periodically watch reruns of *The Andy Griffith Show*. Unlike many of today's programs, the oldies seem to contain practical, life-enhancing messages. In one episode, Sheriff Andy Taylor decides to invite his spinster Aunt Bee to live with Opie and him. Following the death of his wife, Andy thought Aunt Bee would add the missing feminine touch to their home.

Opie doesn't share Andy's sentiments and questioned Aunt Bee coming to "replace" his mother. Andy devised a plan to help Opie accept the idea. He invited Aunt Bee to go fishing and frog-catching with them. Opie would then have a chance to get to know her and hopefully bond with her. Unfortunately, Aunt Bee failed miserably at fishing, couldn't catch a frog, and later revealed her lack of football skills.

Later that night, after Opie was in bed, Aunt Bee asked Andy to take her to the bus station. Opie heard her crying beneath his bedroom window and realized she was leaving. He jumped out of bed, rushed downstairs, ran to the truck, and exclaimed, "We can't let her go, Pa. She needs us. She can't even catch frogs, take fish off the hook, or throw a football. We've got to take care of her, or she'll never make it."

Love springs to life when we realize that the benefit of our relationships is not what we will receive from someone else. We need other people because of our weaknesses; they need us to complement their lives by infusing our strengths with their weaknesses. The process for creating healthy, mutually beneficial relationships unveils this realization: love is best expressed when we fill the void in someone's life. By doing so, we expand the value of our own lives.

Although Sheriff Andy Taylor acted from a pure motive of wanting a feminine influence in their home, it was Opie who delivered the punch line, "We've got to take care of her, or she'll never make it."

Although love may not be reciprocated, our lives will not remain the same when we commit to filling a vacuum in others' lives.

> Love cures people," said "both the ones who give it and the ones who receive it.
>
> Karl Menninger [2]

Chapter 3

MAKING ACTS OF LOVE NO
MATTER HOW WE FEEL

Happy marriages begin when we marry the ones we love, and
they blossom when we love the ones we marry.

—Tom Mullen[1]

D R. JOYCE BROTHERS TELLS THE story of a judge trying to
change the mind of a woman filing for divorce. "You're 92,"
he said. "Your husband is 94. You've been married for 73
years. Why give up now?" "Our marriage has been on the rocks for
quite a while," the woman explained, "but we decided to wait until
the children died."[2]

Dr. Robert Taylor, co-author of *Couples—The Art of Staying
Together*, said "We're now living in the age of disposability: Use it
once, and throw it away. Over the past decade, there has developed a
feeling that relationships are equally disposable."[3]

The throwaway culture in which we live seems intent on throwing
out the principle that marriage is a commitment requiring effort.

A *U.S. News & World Report* study reveals the biggest reason couples split up. It is the "inability to talk honestly with each other, to bare their souls, and to treat each other as their best friend."[4]

Maybe you are familiar with this type of scenario. Your spouse complains, "You never tell me you love me anymore." Taking the hint, you mumble, "Of course I love you." You say that while thinking, "Silly, I wouldn't be living with you if I didn't love you. If anything ever changes, you'll be the first to know." Why don't we just respond with a warm kiss and say, "I'm sorry I haven't told you lately how much I love you."

The great psychologist, Dr. George W. Crane, said in his famous book *Psychology Applied*: "Remember, motions are the precursors of emotions. You can't control the latter directly but only through your choice of motions or actions... To avoid this all too common tragedy (marital difficulties and misunderstandings) become aware of the true psychological facts. Go through the proper motions each day and you'll soon begin to feel the corresponding emotions! Just be sure you and your mate go through those motions of dates and kisses, the phrasing of sincere daily compliments, plus the many other little courtesies and you need not worry about the emotion of love. You can't act devoted for very long without feeling devoted."[5]

When you treat your spouse as the most important person in your life, you will begin feeling it, believing it, and enjoying it. What can you do this week to turn acts into love no matter what your emotions are telling you?

On the dance floor as in life, you're only as good as your partner.
—Robin Marantz Henig[6]

Chapter 4

WHAT DOES LOVE LOOK LIKE?

What does love look like? It has the hand to help others. It has the feet to hasten to the poor and needy. It has the eyes to see misery and want. It has the ears to hear the sighs and sorrows of men. That is what love looks like.

—Saint Augustine[1]

MUCH HAS BEEN WRITTEN *ABOUT* love, but maybe not enough to help us understand *how to* love. I know this is elementary. We need the reminder, though. So, stick with me. Love is more than hugs, kisses, and affection. It transcends the emotional feelings that are usually considered love. Love is demonstrated by an attitude of sensitivity and concern; love is expressed through sincere actions. The emotion of love surfaces and grows from there—it is a result, not a cause.

Let me make this simple. "You can't put a price tag on love," said Melanie Clark, "but you can on all its accessories."[2] Activating the "accessories" of love requires us to eliminate the baggage of pettiness, jealousy, resentment, and judgment. That way, we can just love. Think and behave as if you love. By loving thinking and loving actions, we expand our ability to express authentic love. Remember, the emotional part of love is achieved when the thinking and acting are activated.

I've enjoyed attending the musical play *Fiddler on the Roof* many times. In one scene, Tevye, seeing the example of his daughters, begins to think about love as a basis for marriage. So after years of marriage, he asks his wife, "Do you love me?" She replies, "For twenty-five years I've washed your clothes, cooked your meals, cleaned the house, given you children, milked your cow. After twenty-five years, why talk about love right now?" But Tevye persists: "Do you love me?" After repeated requests, Tevye's wife was only able to respond, "I suppose I do."[3]

"Do you love me?" In the ideal world, this question would be unnecessary. In the real world, countless people yearn to hear the words, "I love you."

Ida Fay Oglesby, writing in the "P.E.O. Record," tells the story of a little eight-year-old girl in a Pennsylvania orphanage who was shy, unattractive, and regarded as a problem. Two other asylums had her transferred, and now this director was seeking some pretext for getting rid of her. One day, someone noticed the little girl was writing a letter. An ironclad rule of the institution was that any communication from a child had to be approved before it was mailed. The next day, the director and her assistant watched the child steal out of the dormitory and slip down to the main gate. Just inside the gate was an old tree with roots showing above the ground. They followed and watched as the child hid the letter in one of the crevices of the root. Carefully looking around, the little girl scurried back to the dormitory.

The director took the note and tore it open. Then, without speaking, she passed the note to her assistant. It read, "To anybody who finds this: I love you."[4]

What a powerful message from the hearts of those hungry to have someone to love and love them back. Can you say it? "I love you."

Alvin Straight lived a few miles from me in Laurens, Iowa, in 1966. His eighty-year-old brother lived several hundred miles away in Mt. Zion, Wisconsin. According to local news reports, Alvin's brother had suffered a stroke. Alvin wanted to see him, but had no transportation. Alvin's eyesight wasn't good enough to have a driver's license, and he refused to take a plane, train, or bus. So Alvin, at age seventy-three, climbed aboard his 1966 John Deere tractor lawn mower and drove it all the way to Mt. Zion, Wisconsin. Now that's devotion.[5]

We should stop viewing the needs of others as inconveniences, irritations, or disruptions to our comfortable lifestyles. Needs are opportunities—opportunities to stretch our ability to give and sharpen our ability to become others-minded.

The following appeared on the editorial page of the *Pasadena Star News* in November of 1985:

> Just about everyone knows the Jim Brady story—the man who, only two months after becoming White House press secretary, was shot in the head during the attempted assassination of President Reagan; and how he has fought his way back from brain surgery and the crippling, enduring damage from the stray bullet.
>
> Not many people know, however, about the ceaseless, selfless, single-minded devoted love of Bob Dahlgren... a man who loved Brady like himself.
>
> A few months ago, Bob Dahlgren died in his sleep at 52 years of age. His death didn't make the morning news. But during the long months following Brady's shooting, it was Dahlgren who took the vigil with Brady's wife, Sarah, through the long series of brain operations. It was Dahlgren and his wife, Suzie, who took Brady's young son, Scott, into their own home through the early days of the ordeal.
>
> It was Dahlgren who arranged the happy hours with Brady's friends by his hospital bedside.
>
> As Brady recovered and returned to a semi-normal life, it was Dahlgren, always Dahlgren, who helped load and unload

his friend from the specially equipped van in which Brady did most of his traveling.

It was Dahlgren who helped Sarah field questions about Brady's health and who spent endless hours keeping friends posted on his condition. It was Dahlgren who helped organize a foundation to assure financial support for the family.

For more than four and a half years after the shooting, Bob Dahlgren devoted virtually all his time to the man he loved. And he did so with little recognition and no hope of getting anything in return. Never did Dahlgren complain. Never did he hesitate when needed.

As Dr. Arthur Kobrine, the surgeon who lived through Brady's long ordeal with him, once said, "Everyone should have a friend like Bob Dahlgren."[6]

Selfless love. It's almost an antiquated concept. Thank goodness for a few practicing servants who demonstrate love beyond understanding.

> Love is like a beautiful flower which I may not touch, but whose fragrance makes the garden a place of delight just the same.
> —Helen Keller[7]

Section Two

ACCEPTANCE

Chapter 5

My Wife Is Always Right

If you are losing a tug-of-war with a tiger, give him the rope before he gets to your arm. You can always buy a new rope.

—Max Gunther[1]

My wife Marty rarely calls me at work. She's made it a habit not to interrupt my day unless there's an emergency or an issue needing immediate attention. As a result, I was a bit anxious returning her call when I returned from a meeting to see a note stating I should call her as soon as possible.

"Hello, sweetheart," I said. "What's up?"

"A bad thing happened," she sheepishly replied. "You know, it's really noisy when you back your car into the garage door."

"Pardon me," I responded, attempting to visualize the scene.

"It's your fault," she continued. "When you left for work this morning, you left your garage door open. I entered the detached garage through your open door and the garage was so well lit from the outside light I didn't realize my door was closed."

"It's my fault?" I chuckled.

"Yes, and now the door is shattered."

Marty and I have laughed about that situation many times. I, of course, continue to remind her that I was not the one in the driver's seat. However, I learned a few important things about potential conflicts, arguments, and marital disputes from this unfortunate incident. First, scratched bumpers and dented trunks can be fixed. They are not worth getting upset about, especially at the expense of harmony.

Secondly, and this is most important, I learned my wife is always right. Now don't get me wrong here. I don't mean to say that I am always wrong, but I carefully choose the issues worth debating. I often recall the advice of Jonathan Kozol: "Pick battles big enough to matter, small enough to win."[2] In other words, decide what issues are worth dying for and which ones you refuse to argue about.

Newspaper and magazine editor H. L. Mencken often drew letters of criticism and outrage from his critiques of American life. He answered every critical letter and handled each one the same way. Mencken simply wrote back, "You may be right."[3] What a marvelous way to diffuse a potentially volatile situation.

For most of us the hardest thing to give is the "giving in." Wanting to win fuels the fire. It causes arguments to digress into lose-lose situations. Maybe that's why Ben Franklin believed, "If you argue and rankle and contradict, you may achieve a victory sometimes; but it will be an empty victory because you will never get your opponent's good will."[4]

Franklin's comment reminds me of the couple traveling down the highway in complete silence. An earlier argument left both unwilling to concede their positions. Passing a barnyard of mules, the husband sarcastically asked, "Are they relatives of yours?"

"Yes," his wife replied. "I married into the family." Ouch!

Sydney J. Harris submitted, "The most important thing in an argument, next to being right, is to leave an escape hatch for your opponent, so that he can gracefully swing over to your side without too much apparent loss of face."[5] That's why I've adopted the attitude that my wife (and any other potential opponent) is always right, even though in the long run my conviction might be proven right.

What's the benefit of taking such an approach? Isn't this escaping, avoiding, and choosing the easy way out? I suppose you could look at it like that. Even though I know there are two sides to every issue— my side, and the side that no informed, intelligent, clear thinking, self-respecting person could possibly hold (only kidding)—any quarrel will not last long if we refuse to continue stirring it up by trying to prove others wrong.

Two men, Jake and Sam, were stuck together on a deserted island. They got along so well that not one cross word passed between them. In fact, their passive behavior made life so harmonious that it became monotonous at times.

One day Jake came up with an idea to break the boredom. "Let's have a heated argument," he suggested, "like people back home often have." Sam responded, "But we don't have anything to argue about." Jake thought for a moment and then suggested, "Let's find a bottle that's washed up on shore and place it on the beach between us. I'll say, 'This bottle is mine!' And you'll say, 'No, it isn't. The bottle is mine!' That will surely get a good argument started."

So, finding a bottle and placing it on the sandy beach between them, Jake exclaimed, "This bottle is mine!" Sam, pausing for moment, responded meekly, "I think, my friend, that the bottle is mine." "Oh, really?" Jake said agreeably. "If the bottle is yours, take it."

It is not humanly possible to carry on an argument between two people when one refuses to argue. So, here's a thought: Let people be right until the heat has subsided and you can discuss the situation rationally.

Two months after our car crashed into the garage door and we had purchased a minivan with a luggage carrier (don't get ahead of me), I got another call at work. "Glenn, you closed your door, but my garage door didn't go up high enough. The luggage carrier hooked the garage door and shattered it. The luggage carrier isn't in great shape either."

You can draw your own conclusions about how this conversation ended.

A married couple was involved in another round of repeated disagreements. The same issue had been bitterly discussed over and over. The wife finally blurted in desperation, "You're impossible!"

Not missing a beat, the husband retorted, "No, I'm *next* to impossible."

Chapter 6

HUGGABLE AND BUGGABLE

At the heart of personality is the need to feel a sense of being
lovable without having to qualify for that acceptance.

—Maurice Wagner[1]

I N MY TEENAGE YEARS, I had a friend, Joe, who was a little shy.
Even in college Joe found it difficult to ask girls out on dates.
Jake, friend who lived down the hall from Joe in the same
dormitory, presented an offer he couldn't refuse. "I've got great
news," Jake said. "I've lined you up with a great date for Saturday
night. Everything is set."

"Who is it?" Joe asked. It turned out to be a friend of Jake's girl-
friend, who was visiting for the weekend. "No thanks," Joe said.
"Blind dates aren't for me."

"No need to worry about this one," my friend reassured me.
"Julie's a terrific girl. And trust me—she's a beauty."

"No," Joe repeated.

"This is a no-fail situation. I'll even give you an out."

Now he had Joe's attention. "How?"

"When we arrive at the dorm to pick them up, wait for her to come to the door. Check her out. If you like what you see, great; we're off for a super evening. But if she looks too ugly, fake an asthma attack. Just say *Aaahhhgggggg,* and grab your throat like you're having trouble breathing. When she asks, 'What's wrong?' You say, 'It's my asthma.' And so we'll call off the date. Just like that. No questions asked. No problem."

Joe was hesitant, but agreed to give it a try. What did he have to lose?

When they got to the door, Joe knocked, and his date came to the door. He took one look at her and couldn't believe his eyes. She was beautiful! He didn't know what to say.

But she did. She took one look at Joe and said, *Aaahhhhgggggg!*

It seems Joe and Jake weren't the only ones with a foolproof plan. Most of us, at one time or another, have been rejected by someone because we weren't smart enough, tall enough, athletic enough, good-looking enough, or whatever. It's tough to feel rejected.

When we unconditionally accept someone, we give them the freedom to be on the outside who they are on the inside. True acceptance will allow us to see the real value of a human being.

Acceptance communicates love and value. It gives people the self-confidence to become all they can be. It also allows them to be who they are until they become what they are capable of becoming.

When Marty and I were dating, I just knew we were going to have a wonderful future together. If only she would make a few changes, that future would be even brighter. I certainly didn't bring the issue up during our dating, and I refrained from talking about it on our honeymoon.

Within a few weeks of settling into marital bliss, though, I decided it was time to bring my suggested changes to the surface. I was bold and stupid enough to verbalize my thoughts at supper one night. I gracefully, lovingly, and rather forthrightly stated my case. Wow, did I learn a ton about marriage that night! I also gleaned a valuable lesson about acceptance.

When we attempt to force people to be who we want them to be, the defensive, stubborn, and hurt qualities emerge. When we give people freedom to refuse to change, we give them the inspiration to consider changing.

Refrain from accepting people based on what they *could be*, *should be*, or *would be* if only they listened to you. Acceptance says "It is what is, and what is is what is." Until we accept unconditionally, we will continually be looking through the filters of musts, shoulds, ought-to's, have-to's, and prejudices.

Eugene Kennedy suggests that, "When someone prizes us just as we are, he or she confirms our existence."[2] Now after thirty-five years of marriage, I'm realizing the value of loving someone regardless of who they are or aren't, what they have or don't have, or for what they do or don't do.

Thank goodness we worked through my naïve insensitivity as a newlywed so I could understand that people, like plants, grow in the soil of acceptance, not in the atmosphere of judgment.

I love the *Peanuts* cartoon where Lucy says to Snoopy, "There are times when you really bug me, but I must admit there are also times when I feel like giving you a big hug." Snoopy replies. "That's the way I am ... huggable and buggable."

It seems to me that Snoopy's response might be an appropriate description for most people in this world—huggable and buggable. Love them anyway.

Chapter 7

CREATING A RELATIONSHIP MASTERPIECE

> A relationship is a living thing. It needs and benefits from the same attention to detail that an artist lavishes on his art.
>
> —David Viscott[1]

T HAT'S A NICE QUOTE FROM David Viscott, isn't it? Let's carry his artistic thought a bit further, though. Consider the following qualities present in relationship masterpieces.

- Start with a blank canvas of acceptance. Permit people to be who they are—not what they could be, should be, or would be if only they listened to you. Accept the imperfections. Celebrate each person's individuality. Acceptance affirms peoples' value, raises self-esteem, and makes them feel comfortable in your presence.

- Artists are masters at the use of primary colors, which create the heart of the finished product.

Mutual trust is one such primary ingredient. We live in an imperfect, messy world made up of imperfect people. Unfortunately, many of us are prone to trusting people only when they prove themselves trustworthy. I tend to believe that if we trust people, they will prove themselves trustworthy. I know that trust can be betrayed, but trust is essential for relationships to develop. Step out. Make an effort to believe in the intrinsic goodness of people. Sure, you might be disappointed, but you will also be blessed.

- Sharing yourself with others is a scary risk. Withholding who we are places a permanent blemish on the relationship canvas. Honest communication stands out in any close friendship. Use discretion, but share your hurts, fears, and failures. Throw in the good stuff with the bad stuff. Just refrain from unnecessary critical, cheap-shot, or hurting comments that are better left unsaid.

I'm sure every artist has a favorite color that tends to find its way into each creation. My favorite relationship ingredient is improving the ability to see the good in people. Tell your friends, family, and coworkers what you like about them. Tell people how thankful you are for them. Recognize their talents, applaud their successes (one of the most difficult actions of human nature), and make others feel important about themselves. Expressing appreciation on every possible occasion is one of the surest ways to boost mutual respect and encourage positive behaviors.

A masterpiece stands out in the viewer's mind when the proper highlights are added. When it comes to relationships, you can move to the next level by:

- Giving more than you get
- Allowing people to have their space
- Maintaining confidentiality
- Giving supportive and positive advice
- Being loyal
- Listening
- Treating others with dignity
- Saying "please" and "thank you"
- Being agreeable
- Accepting others' opinions
- Forgiving wrongs committed

Quality relationships are fulfilling. Relationships don't fail to become beautiful experiences because they are wrong, but because most people don't want to invest what it takes to create an original. To evaluate how effective you are in creating a relationship masterpiece, just ask yourself, "If I were my friend, would I enjoy the artistic strokes (qualities) I experience being with me?"

> I am loyal in relationships. Any relationship. When I go out with my mom I don't look at other moms and say, "Oooh, I wonder what her macaroni and cheese tastes like."
>
> —Gary Shandling[2]

Chapter 8

A Proposition for You

Whoever thinks marriage is a 50-50 proposition doesn't know the half of it.

—Franklin P. Jones[1]

OUR MONTHLY CARD CLUB TENDED to stray from the bridge game we came to play to conversations about local news, our children's activities, and sports events. One Saturday night a discussion ensued about marriage, men's irritating habits (from the women's perspective), and women's misconceptions about men (from the men's viewpoint). It was a light-hearted, give-and-take oral debate that digressed into a competition to see who could share the most cynical philosophy.

My favorite bantering came from a happily married couple with a great sense of humor.

He indicated the key to their model marriage: "My wife and I understand each other. I don't try to run her life, and I don't try to run mine."

Not to be outdone, his wife responded; "The real secret to us staying married such a long time is simple; one of us talks, and the other doesn't listen."

That isn't very funny to the many marriages seeking help. I remember my senior year of college when I took a class entitled "Marriage and the Family." I wasn't dating anyone at the time but I thought, "Why not prepare for future possibilities?" The professor was an entertaining person, and he livened up the lectures by offering ample personal examples from his own life. At the time, I questioned the validity of his stories. Now that I've been married twenty-five years, I understand how even the most outlandish stories could be true.

He began his lecture one day with this bold statement: "The secret of a successful marriage is this: marriage is not a 50-50 proposition. A 50-50 proposition is one where nobody is giving anything."

"Rather, the secret of a happy marriage is 60-40. The husband gives in 60 percent of the time and expects his wife to give in 40 percent of the time. The wife gives in 60 percent of the time and expects her husband to give in 40 percent of the time. In a 60-40 proposition, you don't clash in the middle and say, 'Now, it's your turn.' Instead, you intersect and overlap, because you're each giving 60 percent." I walked out of that classroom, along with seventy-five other students and never thought about the 60-40 proposition again, except of course when it appeared on the final exam.

I'm not sure there is any magic formula for a successful marriage, but I remain intrigued by the concept of always giving a little more than the other person. There is some truth in the old saying, "Marriage is an empty box. It remains empty unless you put more in than you take out."

There are no doubt a multitude of attitudes, abilities, and opinions about what makes a marriage work. In fact, I've pulled together a few tidbits of marriage wisdom. I thought you might enjoy a wide spectrum of perspectives on the joys of tying the knot. Some of the ideas provide wisdom, while others are intended to offer a bit of levity.

The difference between a successful marriage and a mediocre one consists of leaving about three things a day unsaid.

—Michelle Gelman[2]

The failure of modern marriage is, in large measure, accounted for by our failure to employ humor in the process of marital adjustment.

—Julius Gordon[3]

Only two things are necessary to keep one's wife happy. First is to let her think she's having her own way. Second is to let her have it.

—Lady Bird Johnson[4]

Marriage is not just spiritual communion and passionate embraces; marriage is also three-meals-a-day and remembering to carry out the trash.

—Dr. Joyce Brothers[5]

A happy wife sometimes has the best husband, but more often makes the best of the husband she has.

—Mark Beltaire[6]

It takes a loose rein to keep a marriage tight.

—John Stevenson[7]

Marriage is popular because it combines the maximum of temptation with the maximum of opportunity.

—George Bernard Shaw[8]

Marriage resembles a pair of shears, so joined that they cannot be separated; often moving in opposite directions, yet always punishing anyone who comes between them.

—Sydney Smith[9]

Marriage should be a duet—when one sings, the other claps.

—Joe Murray[10]

I've never thought about divorce. I've thought about murder, but never divorce.

—Dr. Joyce Brothers[11]

Marriage is like vitamins, we supplement each other's minimum daily requirements.

—Kathy Mohnke[12]

Sometimes I wonder if men and women really suit each other. Perhaps they should live next door and just visit now and then.

—Katherine Hepburn[13]

Keep your eyes wide open before marriage, half shut afterward.

—Benjamin Franklin[14]

One of the reasons I made the most important decision of my life—to marry George Bush—is because he made me laugh. It's true, sometimes we laugh through our tears, but that shared laughter has been one of our strongest bonds.

—Barbara Bush[15]

In biblical times, a man could have as many wives as he could afford. Just like today.

—Abigail Van Buren[16]

There is no more lovely, friendly, and charming relationship, communion, or company than a good marriage.

—Martin Luther[17]

People are always asking couples whose marriage has endured at least a quarter of a century for their secret for success. Actually, it is no secret at all. I am a forgiving woman. Long ago, I forgave my husband for not being Paul Newman.

—Erma Bombeck[18]

Lots of people have asked me what Gracie and I did to make our marriage work. It's simple—we didn't do anything. I think the trouble with a lot of people is that they work too hard at staying married. They make a business out of it. When you work too hard at a business you get tired; and when you get tired you get grouchy; and when you get grouchy you start fighting; and when you start fighting, you're out of business.

—George Burns[19]

An archeologist is the best husband any woman can have. The older she gets, the more he is interested in her!

—Agatha Christie[20]

Husband: "Honey, you've got to admit, men have better judgment than women."

Wife: "I couldn't agree more—you married me, and I married you."

The trouble with some women is that they get all excited about nothing—and then marry him.

—Cher[21]

Some people ask the secret of our long marriage. We take time to go to a restaurant two times a week. A little candlelight, dinner, soft music and dancing. She goes Tuesdays. I go Fridays.

—Henny Youngman[22]

We have a picture of the perfect partner, but we marry an imperfect person. Then we have two options. Tear up the picture and accept the person, or tear up the person and accept the picture.

—J. Grant Howard, Jr.[23]

It destroys one's nerves to be amiable every day to the same human being.

—Benjamin Disraeli[24]

Familiarity breeds contempt—and children.

—Mark Twain[25]

The most important thing a father can do for his children is to love their mother.

—Rev. Theodore Hesburgh[26]

More marriages might survive if the partners realized that sometimes the better comes after the worse.

—Doug Larson[27]

After winning an argument with his wife, the wisest thing a man can do is apologize.

—Ann Landers[28]

We sleep in separate rooms, we have dinner apart, we take separate vacations—we're doing everything we can to keep our marriage together.

—Rodney Dangerfield[29]

In marrying, you vow to love one another. Would it not be better for your happiness if you vowed to please one another?

—Stanislaus Leszcynski[30]
1763 King of Poland

Section Three

FORGIVENESS

Chapter 9

KEEP YOUR BRIDGES IN GOOD REPAIR

He that cannot forgive others breaks the bridge over which he must pass himself; for every man has need to be forgiven.

—Thomas Fuller[1]

L OVE AND ACCEPTANCE CAN ONLY reach their potential if we learn the beauty of forgiveness.

General Oglethorpe once said to John Wesley, "I never forgive and I never forget." To which Wesley responded, "Then, sir, I hope you never sin."[2]

The general probably never experienced the load-lifting action of forgiveness. To forgive someone means to let go. Once you forgive, emotional baggage—tension, unresolved conflicts, mistreatment— is lifted. Robin Casarjian, author of *Forgiveness: A Bold Choice for a Peaceful Heart,* managed to forgive the man who raped her. She said, "Once you forgive, you are no longer emotionally handcuffed to the person who hurt you."[3] That is freedom!

"You have a tremendous advantage over the person who slanders you or does you a willful injustice," declared Napoleon Hill. "You have it within your power to forgive that person."[4]

Are you angry with someone who has offended you? You have two choices: stay angry or forgive. Anger pulls you down. Forgiveness provides you the power to get on with life. Let it go.

Do you carry grudges? Grudges are simply a buildup of resentment produced by an unwillingness to genuinely forgive. We can't "bury the hatchet" with the handle sticking out. Let it go.

Have you ever said, "I'll forgive, but I can't forget"? That is only superficial forgiveness that allows us to continue to wallow in self-pity. The quickest way to forget is to quit dwelling on the wrong done to you. Let it go.

The American Red Cross was founded by a pioneering woman named Clara Barton who was widely known for her forgiving spirit. A friend once brought up an injustice done to her years before. When Barton failed to respond to the effort to relive this event, the friend persisted, "Don't you remember how much that person hurt you?" "No," Clara Barton cheerfully responded. "I distinctly remember forgetting that."[5]

To proactively forgive the past, quit dwelling on the hurt. By not reliving the situation over and over you will gain peace and victory over the incident.

If you want to maintain the bridges that sustain relationships but sense some repair work is needed, consider the following suggestions.

- **Be the first to ask forgiveness.** Whether you have hurt someone or been mistreated, be the first to say, "Please forgive me if I've done anything to hurt our relationship." This action allows you to let go and get on with your life.

- **Rebuild your thoughts.** The mind is a marvelous mechanism. The thoughts we hold in this massive human computer will dominate our lives. Although not an easy task, discipline yourself not to dwell on the situation or the bitterness, blame, or hurt that can saturate your mind.

- **Pray.** I am rarely capable of genuine forgiveness without divine intervention. Relying on God to help me deal with the pain, the person, and the process of healing replaces the human tendency of revenge with release.

- **Write a letter.** Expressing your feelings in writing, without placing judgment or blame, can be a signif-icant bridge from pain to peace. Simply commu-nicating your heart signals a desire to achieve resolution. Whether or not you ever send the letter, writing it contains its own value.

- **Focus on the future.** Wallowing in the mire of the past destroys the bridge to the future. Tomorrow can never be lived to the fullest when we are consumed with the uncontrollable past.

Elbert Hubbard wrote, "A retentive memory may be a good thing, but the ability to forget is the true token of greatness. [Successful people forget. They know the past is irrevocable. They're running a race. They can't afford to look behind. Their eye is on the finish line.] Magnanimous people forget. They're too big to let little things disturb them. They forget easily. If anyone does them wrong, they consider the source and keep cool. It's only small people who cherish revenge. Be a good forgetter. Business dictates it, and success demands it."[6]

Forgiveness allows you to be free from the nightmares of the past and to reclaim your dreams for the future.

- **Replace selfishness with unconditional love.** Old Pete was in bad health and death seemed immi-nent. For years there had been a thorn of bitterness with Joe, formerly one of his best friends. Wanting to clear the air, Pete sent word for Joe to come and see him.

When Joe arrived, Pete told him that he couldn't face eternity knowing their relationship had been destroyed. Pete painfully and reluctantly apologized for the hurtful things he had said and done. He also assured Joe that he forgave him for his actions. The two old friends shook hands, and everything seemed fine until Joe turned to go and Pete said, "If I get better, none of this counts."

Saying, "I forgive you" and then placing conditions on our forgiveness equates with not forgiving at all. It's tough to remove our selfish motives and refrain from resurrecting past grievances when frictions arise.

I'm reminded here of the lady who sought marriage counseling.

The counselor asked her what seemed to be the source of their difficulty.

"Whenever we get into an argument," the lady said, "my husband becomes historical."

"Don't you mean hysterical?" the counselor responded.

"No, I mean historical! He always brings up the past."

Emotional problems and relational stress will continue as long as forgiveness hinges on the past. Total forgiveness requires unconditional love.

Forgiveness is a basic requirement for relationships to mature and reap positive results. Forgiveness remains the bridge we must cross in order to enter brighter tomorrows. Remember the words of Martin Luther King, Jr.: "Forgiveness is not an occasional act; it is a permanent attitude."[7]

> Ninety percent of the art of living consists of getting along with people you cannot stand.
> —Samuel Goldwyn[8]

Chapter 10

PLACING PEOPLE IN
PROPER PERSPECTIVE

The primary joy of life is the acceptance, approval, sense of appreciation and companionship of our human comrades. Many men do not understand that the need for fellowship is really as deep as the need for food, and so they go throughout life accepting many substitutes for genuine, warm, simple relatedness.

—Joshua Loth Liebman[1]

BARBARA BUSH WAS NOT WELLESLEY College's first choice as their 1990 graduation commencement speaker. Some of the seniors didn't view her as a role model for the issues facing today's modern woman.

"To honor Barbara Bush as a commencement speaker," they protested, "is to honor a woman who has gained recognition through the achievements of her husband, which contradicts what we have been taught the past four years."[2]

The first lady handled the accusations in her classy style; she didn't allow the protests to offend or intimidate her. Mrs. Bush spoke from her heart about the fulfillment she had experienced from her traditional values. She offered this advice in her commencement address:

> Cherish your human connections, your relationships with friends and family. For several years, you've had impressed upon you the importance to your career of dedication and hard work. This is true, but as important as your obligations as a doctor, lawyer, or business leader will be, you are a human being first, and those human connections—with spouses, with children, with friends—are the most important investments you will ever make. At the end of your life, you will never regret not having passed one more test, not winning one more verdict, or not closing one more deal. You will regret time not spent with a husband, a friend, a child, or a parent.[3]

The first lady addressed the heart of living. All of our personal and professional endeavors are made sweeter, richer, and more satisfying by sharing them with others. As Antoine de Saint-Exupery wrote, "There is no hope or joy except in human relationships."[4]

Too often, what should matter most in our lives receives the least attention. Battles with the almighty dollar, pursuing selfish interests, attaining that next promotion, or closing a deal are empty pursuits without the human element. It's easy to forget that our relationships are what encourage the heart and nourish the soul.

Harold Kushner, in *When All You've Ever Wanted Isn't Enough*, wrote: "A life without people, without the same people day after day, people who belong to us, people who will be there for us, people who need us and whom we need in return, may be very rich in other things, but in human terms, it is no life at all."[5]

A life without relationships limits the value of everything we do. Regardless of the pressures you feel to succeed in our what's-in-it-for-me society, don't make the mistake of placing value on only those activities and goals that enhance your paycheck. Maintain the proper perspective of people. You will never regret it.

Only you can know how much you can give to every aspect of your life. Try to decide what is the most important. And if you do, then only occasionally will you resent or regret the demands of the marriage, the career, or the child, or the staying.

—Barbara Walters[6]

Chapter 11

BE WILLING TO SAY "I'M SORRY"

The most deadly of all sins is the mutilation of a child's spirit.
—Erik H. Erikson[1]

I CHERISH SO MUCH ABOUT OUR children. Through my many years of parenting, this is what I treasure the most: each relationship.

Oh, I admit it's nice when they score points in a basketball game or gracefully perform a dance routine. I'm pleased when their report cards reveal above-average scores, or when I observe the effort put into a school project. And of course it's flattering when people comment how nice they look or how respectful they are.

But what really trips my trigger and renews my parental energy—after returning from a speaking trip, or working on a free throw shot, playing taxi driver, or setting curfew—is a loving smile, a hug, a high five, and the four cherished words: "I love you, Dad."

I'm keenly aware how my actions, words, tone of voice, or nonverbals affect the loving, caring, and mutually respectful relationship we enjoy. And, I've failed at times as a father to uphold my end of the responsibility. There have been situations when I crushed my children's spirits.

When my son was in the sixth grade, another dad and I agreed to coach a traveling basketball team. Along with our two sons, we invited ten other boys to enjoy the experience with us.

It didn't take long for me to realize that the definition of a father-coach is someone who expects his son to be everything he wasn't. I upheld high and sometimes unrealistic expectations. I even found it easy to justify my demands by attempting to motivate my son to be the best he could be. However, during one game I overstepped my parental privileges.

The game was already won. The boys fought courageously to overcome a major point deficit to hold a comfortable lead with thirty-seven seconds left in the game. Out of nowhere Matt (my son) stole the ball, dribbled the length of the court, and *missed* an uncontested lay-up.

I chose to release my accumulated tension from the game on my son for missing that lay-up. The shot meant nothing. We had won the game and advanced to the finals. Matt played with heart and gave his all, yet he blew that simple lay-up. I let him know in no uncertain terms how disappointed I was and how ridiculous it was for him to miss such a simple shot.

The joy of winning drained from his face. He stood motionless and speechless as Dad continued to drain the power from his self-esteem battery. I knew I'd blown it, but I continued to justify my outburst and dig myself into a deeper hole.

The next hours waiting for the championship game were long and quiet. Matt was hurting inside, and I was full of guilt. There was little question that I needed my son's forgiveness.

Sitting in our van outside the gymnasium, I slowly turned to look into Matt's fearful and discouraged face. "Matt, I was wrong," I began. "I'm sorry for blowing up at you. You worked hard in that game, and I failed to recognize you for all the good things you did. Please forgive me."

It was then that Matt touched my heart, and my eyes filled with tears. "It's okay, Dad. I know you love me."

Thanks to my son, I could walk into the championship game with a clear conscience, a repaired heart, and a softer spirit.

We lost the championship game by one point, but I came out of that tournament a winner. My son had forgiven me.

The only way to heal a damaged spirit is to swallow the parental pride and say, "I'm sorry. I was wrong. Please forgive me." Failure to bring healing when you've been unfair or hurtful can breed anger for years to come.

When was the last time you told your child, "I'm sorry for anything I have ever said or done that has hurt you"?

> If you were to ask what is the hardest task in the world, you might think of some muscular feat, some acrobatic challenge, some chore to be done on the battlefield or the playing field. Actually, however, there is nothing which we find more arduous than saying, "I was wrong."
>
> —*Sunshine* magazine[2]

Chapter 12

LET GO OF THE PAST

Forgiveness is the key that unlocks the door of resentment and the handcuffs of hate. It is a power that breaks the chains of bitterness and the shackles of selfishness.

—William Arthur Ward[1]

I WAS YOUNG WHEN THE MOVIE *The Hiding Place* was released. The impact of this dramatic story detailing one family's efforts to hide Jews in Holland from the Nazis and their later suffering in a Nazi death camp remains with me many years later. Corrie ten Boom and her family were featured in the movie. She later returned to that death camp in Germany to deliver a message of forgiveness to a group of German people. Little did she know that experience would test her forgiving spirit.

In her book, *Tramp for the Lord*, Corrie recalled,

> The place was Ravensbruck and the man who was making his way forward had been a guard—one of the most cruel guards.
>
> Now he was in front of me, hand thrust out: "A fine message, Fraulein! How good it is to know that, as you say, all our sins are at the bottom of the sea!"

46

And I, who had spoken so glibly of forgiveness, fumbled in my pocketbook rather than take that hand. He would not remember me, of course—how could he remember one prisoner among those thousands of women?

But I remembered him. I was face-to-face with one of my captors, and my blood seemed to freeze.

"You mentioned Ravensbruck in your talk," he was saying. "I was a guard there." No, he did not remember me.

"But since that time," he went on, "I have become a Christian. I know that God has forgiven me for the cruel things I did there, but I would like to hear it from your lips as well. Fraulein,"—again the hand came out—"will you forgive me?"

And I stood there—I whose sins had again and again to be forgiven—and could not forgive. Betsie [Corrie's sister] had died in that place. Could He erase her slow terrible death simply for the asking?

It could have been many seconds that he stood there—hand held out—but to me it seemed hours as I wrestled with the most difficult thing I had ever had to do.[2]

Visualize that scene in your mind. Try to feel what Corrie ten Boom felt, although I doubt we can come close to the inner struggle she was experiencing. How could this man expect to be forgiven for the cruel and inhumane treatment he delivered? How could he have the audacity to suggest that Corrie offer him release from his past?

Mahatma Gandhi believed this: "The weak can never forgive. Forgiveness is the attribute of the strong."[3]

Corrie ten Boom was a strong person. A gallant believer in the benefits of two-way forgiveness, she forgave. I believe Corrie ten Boom not only released that prison guard from a past of regret, but also I believe she also made a critical leap forward in her own faith and inner healing. She allowed herself to move forward.

We all experience various ups and downs in our relationships. Some of us have been hurt by those we love the most. Others live in a daily environment of put-downs and disrespect. There are people who dread an encounter with someone who has broken their spirit. Some folks shudder every time they think about a person who has destroyed their trust.

Hurt people are everywhere. Relationships are in shambles. Loneliness is rampant. Undeserved unfairness, injustice, or even abandonment happens. Isolation becomes the escape for many.

There are many people out there waiting to hear the words, "I forgive you," while many victims are finding a way to pay them back in revenge. We've become a nation obsessed with getting even. How else can you explain the headlines in our newspapers? Neighbors threatening neighbors. Lawsuits for the most ridiculous reasons. Shootings in schools. Grudges leading to beatings. Stalkings. Parents kidnapping their own children from the other parent. The list is depressing.

Earnest Hemingway, in his short story "The Capital of the World," tells of a father and his teenage son living in Spain. Through a series of events, their relationship became strained and eventually shattered. The boy opted to flee from his home. The father began a desperate search for his lost, rebellious yet loved son.

Running out of options, the father resorted to placing an ad in the Madrid newspaper. His son's name was Paco, a common name in Spain. The ad simply read: "Dear Paco, meet me in front of the Madrid newspaper office tomorrow at noon. All is forgiven. I love you."

Hemingway then provides us with an incredible picture and message. The next day at noon in front of the newspaper office there were eight hundred Pacos all seeking forgiveness.[4]

Countless people in this world wait to be forgiven. There are just as many who could benefit from forgiving. Show me a person who lives in peace with themselves and others, and I'll show you a person who freely and sincerely forgives. Forgiveness is the bridge we all must cross to leave pain, heartache, despair, anger, and hurt behind. It takes a tremendous willingness to risk, with courage and humility, crossing that bridge. But on the other side, peace, joy, love, and comfort await us. To fully forgive allows us to fully live.

So often people dwell on past bitterness and present themselves as martyrs for having endured. Unfortunately, the feelings of anger, mistrust, and resentment seep into their other relationships and poison what could otherwise be a healthy experience. There is only one cure, and that is to forgive and let it go. Brian Tracy suggests that we "issue a blanket pardon to everyone for everything that they have ever done to hurt you in any way."[5]

In no way do I suggest forgiveness is easy. In fact, Laurence Sterne said, "Only the brave know how to forgive... a coward never forgave; it [was] not in his nature."[6] I figure if Corrie ten Boom could muster the courage to forgive the man responsible for her torment, who am I to pass eternal judgment and harbor lifelong resentment for the comparatively insignificant abuses I've experienced?

Years ago, our high school put on the play *Joseph and the Amazing Technicolor Dreamcoat*. In addition to the enjoyment of watching my son perform onstage, I was once again reminded how the real biblical character was mistreated and hated by his brothers. Joseph was a young visionary who often had dreams about the future. What really irked his brothers was one dream in which Joseph saw himself ruling over them. The brothers didn't take kindly to that. The brothers were also a bit jealous about their father's visible favoritism toward Joseph that included the gift of a multi-colored coat. Joseph's brothers figured enough was enough, so they grabbed him, tossed him into a pit, and sold him into slavery.

Joseph endured the rejection of his own blood relatives while working for a wealthy Egyptian whose wife had a thing for Joseph and continually tried to seduce him. He was wrongly accused and imprisoned. Joseph was later released, gained favor with the king, offered power and privileges second only to the king, and was ultimately highly esteemed by others.

Here's where the story gets interesting. Years after his brothers' betrayal, they traveled to Egypt during a time of famine looking for help from the government. Little did they know that their younger brother Joseph was in charge of those services. Joseph immediately recognized his brothers, but it was clear to Joseph that they did not recognize him. Joseph possessed the power to get sweet revenge, but what did he do? Joseph rose above past circumstances, refused to cast blame, and responded to his brothers in love, acceptance, and forgiveness. (See Genesis 45.)

Letting go of the past provides a springboard for our lives to move into the future. Corrie ten Boom did it, Joseph did it, and so can you.

In *Angels Don't Die*, Patti Davis shared the impact on her of the attitude of her father, President Ronald Reagan, after the 1982 assassination attempt on his life.

> The following day my father said he knew his physical healing was directly dependent on his ability to forgive John Hinckley. By showing me that forgiveness is the key to everything, including physical health and healing, he gave me an example of Christ-like thinking.[7]

> Doing an injury puts you below your enemy; revenging one makes you but even with him; forgiving it sets you above him.
> —Benjamin Franklin[8]

Section Four

KINDNESS

Chapter 13

ENLARGE YOUR CIRCLE OF INFLUENCE

You can make more friends in two months by becoming really interested in other people than you can in two years by trying to get other people interested in you.

—Dale Carnegie[1]

HOW LARGE IS YOUR POCKET PC's memory? How many names are saved in your Outlook? How many people have you deemed important enough to list in the telephone and address section of your day planner? When is the last time you added someone to your list of valued resources or included a new name for your blog?

How many times have you entered the room of a meeting, seminar, social gathering, or community event and quickly scanned the audience to find someone you knew? How many interesting people did you overlook by cozying up and attaching yourself to only "known" people?

Not only is it advisable to align yourself with activities and a lifestyle that breeds a broader vision of life, but it is also equally important to align yourself with an ever expanding circle of influence. Surround yourself with exceptional people who have discovered the world in a way different than you have.

Most of us become so comfortable with our acquaintances. We play golf with the same foursome, associate with the same people at work, have lunch with our select network, attend social events with a small inner circle, and enjoy philosophical conversation with those we have repeated the same conversations over and over.

Let's change that. Create and capitalize on every window of opportunity possible to get acquainted with at least one new person every week. Step out of your comfort zone, and introduce yourself to someone.

When you fill up at a gas station, strike up a conversation with the person behind the counter. Ask your next server at a restaurant about the most interesting situation he or she dealt with that day. When ordering over the phone from a catalog, question the person taking your order about the things he or she enjoys most about his or her job. Make contact with six people in your community, and ask them to tell you about their profession.

The opportunities are endless. You must begin seeing every person you encounter as an opportunity to learn, grow, and expand your knowledge.

Blast through the barriers of shyness, fear, being self-conscious, or even apathetic to show others how interested you are in their lives and experiences. You'll be amazed how accommodating people can be when you express a sincere interest in them. It takes a variety of people to challenge us, encourage us, promote us, and most of all, help us achieve a broader dimension of ourselves.

> I am going to be meeting people today who talk too much—people who are selfish, egotistical, ungrateful. But I wouldn't be surprised or disturbed, for I can't imagine a world without such people.
>
> —Marcus Aurelius[2]

Strange is our situation here upon Earth. Each of us comes for a short visit, not knowing why, yet sometimes seeming to divine a purpose. From the standpoint of daily life, however, there is one thing we do know: that we are here for the sake of others...for the countless unknown souls with whose fate we are connected by a bond of sympathy. Many times a day, I realize how much my outer and inner life is built upon the labors of people, both living and dead, and how earnestly I must exert myself in order to give in return as much as I have received.

—Albert Einstein[3]

Chapter 14

BEWARE OF BECOMING A FAULT-FINDER

Our worst fault is our preoccupation with the faults of others.
—Kahlil Gibran[1]

REMEMBER THE CHARLIE BROWN CARTOON strips? Charlie Brown suffered from the "I can't do anything right" syndrome. Lucy was always there to remind him of the error of his ways.

On one occasion Lucy put her hands on her hips and said, "You, Charlie Brown, are a foul ball in the line drive of life! You're in the shadow of your own goalposts! You are a miscue! You are three putts on the eighteenth green! You are a seven-ten split in the tenth frame! You are a dropped rod and reel in the lake of life! You are a missed free throw, a shanked nine iron, and a called third strike! Do you understand? Have I made myself clear?"[2]

The tendency to be a Lucy is tempting. How easy it is to point out to people what they aren't, haven't been, or never will become. Whether you are raising a family, running a company, or building a relationship, be sensitive to the words of wisdom from Will Rogers:

"There is nothing as easy as denouncing. It don't take much to see that something is wrong, but it does take some eyesight to see what will put it right again."[3]

Kahlil Gibran's comment says a lot: "Our worst fault is our preoccupation with the faults of others."[4]

In most cases, criticism is a futile and destructive process. It forces people to be defensive, and it usually causes them to make attempts at justifying their actions. Insensitivity will bruise pride and reduce people's sense of importance. It causes resentment within relationships.

Have you thought lately about someone you would like to change, control, or improve? Fine. Begin with yourself. It has been said that most of us find it difficult to accept the imperfections in others that we possess ourselves. It's uncomfortable to watch people displaying the same negative qualities we ourselves have been unable to overcome. Confucius once said: "Don't complain about the snow on your neighbor's roof when your own doorstep is unclean."[5] Attempting first to improve ourselves will provide us with a greater degree of tolerance concerning the weaknesses or undesirable traits of others.

The late John Wanamaker once reflected, "I learned thirty years ago that it is foolish to scold. I have enough trouble overcoming my own limitations without fretting over the fact that God has not seen fit to distribute evenly the gift of intelligence."[6]

Concentrating on me first—with my heavy load of shortcomings, faults, and areas needing improvement—enhances my ability to accept the limitations of others.

If you're thinking, "I wish my spouse/boss/friend would read this…" then the message hasn't soaked in. Avoiding a fault-finding lifestyle is your responsibility. An upbeat, encouraging, nourishing relationship begins with you.

Most fault-finding begins with something like this: "Perhaps I shouldn't say this, but…." Another common way to slip into critical remarks is by prefacing our comments with, "I don't mean to criticize, but…." And then we go on to do what? Criticize. Once we've shared our inspired observations, we justify them by saying, "I was only trying to help."

There is a huge gap between destructive criticism and constructive feedback that grows out of a sincere desire to enrich someone's life. You can make a positive difference in someone's life by avoiding a fault-finding approach and endorsing a spirit of affirmation and help. Consider these approaches:

1. Uphold people's self-esteem. "I give up." "What's the use?" "I never do anything right." These are common feelings of people who feel defeated and deflated by personal attacks.

The apostle Paul wrote to the church in Rome: "Why then do you criticize your brother's actions, why do you try to make him look small?" (See Romans 14.)

Looking small hurts. People can tell us all day long how wonderful we are and how great it is to be friends. Then one person criticizes us, and we are devastated. The human mind recorder plays that tape over and over, forgetting the positives and bemoaning the one critical comment.

Be kind. Be gentle. Never forget that a person's spirit is easily crushed. Let people know how much you care for them before offering corrective advice. After giving negative feedback, offer additional affirmation of your respect, love, and concern for the person.

2. Focus on abilities rather than vulnerabilities. I've never met a person who has the ability to do anything worthwhile while using their weaknesses. Tell people what you like about their performance before suggesting improvement. Find something, no matter how small or insignificant it might seem, that you can compliment. It's much easier to swallow criticism that is preceded by a sincere affirmation of what we do well.

3. Check your motives. Criticism is often an attempt to raise our own self-concept by comparing our faults to the weaknesses we observe in others. If I can point out some glitch in your life then mine doesn't look so bad. When I am especially sensitive to an area in my life that needs adjustment, it is wise for me to be careful about what I am looking for in others. Lord Chesterfield said, "People hate those who make them feel their own inferiority."[7] Ouch! Are you really trying to help, or are you motivated by an effort to boost your own ego? Thomas Cogswell Upham adds a quote by Madame de la Motte Guyon, "It is often our own imperfection which makes us reprove the imperfection of others; a sharp-sighted self-love of our own which cannot pardon the self-love of others."[8]

Alice Duer Miller advised: "If it's painful for you to criticize your friends—you're safe in doing it. But if you take the slightest pleasure in it—that's the time to hold your tongue."[9]

4. Keep your attitude in check. Fault-finding communicates the attitude, "I want you to feel as miserable as I am." We don't actually say that to someone, but think about it. When do you criticize others the most—when life is flowing along like a dream? Probably not. How about when you are experiencing a trying day? Being sensitive to your emotions will help you refrain from communicating an attitude that, because you're a crab, someone is about to get dumped on. Refuse to blame others for the way you feel.

5. Offer assistance. "What can I do to help?" That is a powerful question. Abraham Lincoln believed, "He has a right to criticize who has a heart to help."[10]

A teenager became an extremely critical backseat driver after completing her driver education course. Finally, her new license arrived, and it was her turn behind the wheel. The roads were wet and slippery, and when she braked at a stop sign, the car began to slide sideways through the intersection toward a parked car.

"Daddy, what do I do?" she shrieked.

"Quick, jump in the back seat," he answered. "You'll think of something."

Don't be a critical backseat driver. Help people look for alternatives. Offer options. Give of yourself. Do whatever you can to help a person be successful.

Fault-finding poisons people's spirits. It chips away at their self-worth. Withdrawal seeks security. Defensiveness surfaces. Trust is broken. Love wilts. Growth, cooperation, love, sensitivity, encouragement, and understanding don't exist in a relationship plagued with criticism. If you persist in pointing out limitations, destruction is imminent.

Discuss unmet expectations honestly and objectively. Offer caring suggestions. Provide educated advice. Encourage people to be the best they can be. Accept people for who they are, mistakes and all.

> A critic is someone who never actually goes to the battle yet who afterwards comes out shooting the wounded.
>
> —Tyne Daly[11]

Chapter 15

DON'T OVERLOOK LITTLE
ACTS OF KINDNESS

At the hour of death, when we come face to face with God, we are going to be judged on love—not how much we have done, but how much love we put into our actions.

—Mother Teresa[1]

MR. AND MRS. DWIGHT MORROW, together with their daughter, Anne [future wife of Charles Lindbergh], called on Governor [Calvin] Coolidge at the Hotel Touraine, in Boston. On the train ride back to New York, several people came into their drawing-room, and Coolidge's name was introduced. Morrow said that Coolidge had Presidential possibilities, but several men disagreed, and one broke out, "No one would like him." Then Anne [age six] spoke up, holding out a finger bound with adhesive tape, "*I* like him. He was the only one that asked about my sore finger." Morrow looked pleased and said, "There's your answer."[2]

Anne had a good point. Maybe asking a little girl about her sore finger isn't necessarily a bona fide qualification for the presidency, but a spirit of kindness is a surefire way to impress others. Kindness, the sincere expression of love, makes the people around you feel loved and valuable.

English author Rita Snowden reflected on a visit she made to a village not far from Dover. She vividly recalled how, as she sat drinking tea at a sidewalk cafe in the afternoon sun of a balmy spring day, she suddenly became aware of a pleasant smell that filled the air. She said it was as though she was suddenly surrounded by flowers.

When Snowden asked where the pleasant aroma was coming from, she was told that it was from the people who worked in a nearby perfume factory. Most of the village's residents worked in a perfume factory in the middle of town. At 4:30, when the workday was over, their clothing was saturated with the perfume scent that accompanied them as they entered the streets.[3]

Opportunities to show kindness abound. If someone were to pay you ten cents for every kindness you ever showed and collect five cents for every unkind word or action, would you be rich or poor?

Flash a smile to those you meet on the street. William Arthur Ward believed, "A warm smile is the universal language of kindness."[4]

Use the precious words *please* and *thank you* at every possible occasion. St. Ambrose suggested that, "No duty is more urgent than that of returning thanks."[5]

Show concern for those inflicted with little hurts and big ones. Allow others to go in front of you in the grocery line (that's a tough one for me). Make it possible for people to change lanes in heavy traffic. Open the door for someone entering the same building as you. Offer a warm greeting to people you meet walking in hotel hallways.

You might be thinking, "Isn't this a bit simplistic?" You're right. But remember what impressed young Anne Morrow. It was a sensitive expression of concern for a bandaged finger that made a positive impression. Simple? Maybe. Effective? No doubt. It's the consistency of our little acts of kindness that cause people to smell a pleasant aroma about us wherever we go.

"Spread your love everywhere you go," encouraged Mother Teresa. "First of all in your own house. Give love to your children, to your wife or husband, to a next door neighbour... Let no one ever come to you without leaving better and happier. Be the living expression of God's kindness; kindness in your face, kindness in your eyes, kindness in your smile, kindness in your warm greeting."[6]

> When we remember our unkindness to friends who have passed beyond the veil, we wish we could have them back again, if only for a moment, so that we could go on our knees to them and say, "Have pity and forgive."
>
> —Mark Twain[7]

Chapter 16

KINDNESS AS A LIFESTYLE

Never lose sight of the fact that the most important yard-stick of your success will be how you treat other people—your family, friends, and coworkers, and even strangers you meet along the way.

—Barbara Bush[1]

I READ A STORY ABOUT A woman who answered the knock on her door to find a man with a sad expression.

"I'm sorry to disturb you," he said, "but I'm collecting money for an unfortunate family in the neighborhood. The husband is out of work, the kids are hungry, the shelves are bare, the utilities will soon be cut off, and worse, they're going to be kicked out of their apartment if they don't pay the rent by this afternoon."

"I'd be happy to help out," said the woman with great concern. "But who are you?"

"I'm the landlord," he replied.

Suffice it to say the landlord was not an enviable example of kindness. At the same time we can probably all relate to times when kindness was used to get our own way or to convince someone to do something that would benefit us. But pure kindness flows from pure motives.

Chuck Wall, a human relations instructor at Bakersfield College in California, was watching a local news program one day when a cliché from a broadcaster caught his attention: "Another random act of senseless violence."

Wall had an idea. He gave an unusual and challenging assignment to his students. They were to do something out of the ordinary to help someone. They were to then write an essay about it.

Wall then dreamed up a bumper sticker that read, "Today, I will commit one random act of senseless KINDNESS...will you?" Students sold the bumper stickers for one dollar each and donated the profits to a county Braille center.

An impressive variety of acts of kindness were performed. One student paid his mother's utility bills. Another student bought thirty blankets from the Salvation Army and took them to homeless people gathered under a bridge.

The idea expanded. Bumper stickers were slapped on all one hundred thirteen county patrol cars. The message was trumpeted from pulpits, in schools, and endorsed by professional associations.

As Chuck Wall reflected on the success of his idea, he commented, "I had no idea our community was in such need of something positive."[2]

It's not just your community, Mr. Wall, that needs random acts of kindness.

After Wausau, Wisconsin was featured as the subject of a negative story on *60 Minutes,* the *Wausau Daily Herald* talked area businesses into co-sponsoring a "Random Acts of Kindness Week."

Businesses, organizations, and individuals were encouraged to perform simple acts of kindness for people they knew or didn't know. The response was gigantic. Over two hundred businesses and organizations participated. The employees of the newspaper wore "Random Acts of Kindness" T-shirts and performed good deeds.

Banks washed car windows in the drive-up lanes. Church groups mowed lawns for people in the neighborhood. Movie theaters gave out free passes to people waiting in line. One individual walked into a restaurant and bought a cup of coffee for every person in the place. The newspaper ran a hotline for people to phone in the acts of kindness they had witnessed. More than five hundred calls were received. The response was so tremendous that the *Wausau Daily Herald* decided to repeat the event the next year.[3]

This week, how about creating a random-acts-of-kindness life-style? Our motto would be, "Every day, in some way, I will show kindness to someone who is not in a position to repay me." We might be amazed at how the idea grows.

> Courtesy is the one coin you can never have too much of or be stingy with.
>
> —John Wanamaker[4]

Section Five

FRIENDSHIP

Chapter 17

PORTRAIT OF A FRIENDSHIP

A friend is someone we can count on for understanding, support, discretions, and, if we're lucky, insight, wisdom, and well-timed foolishness.

—John R. O'Neil[1]

REFLECT ON THE FOLLOWING VIEW of friendship from the *Book of Sunshine*. Those who turn their radio dials to sports commentaries will perhaps have relished this human interest story of President Dwight Eisenhower.

It occurred in a little town in Kansas, where Dwight Eisenhower spent his boyhood days. He was a comely lad, strong and virile, filled with the spirit of an athlete. He chose boxing as his pastime, and his ambition and skilled technique soon made him the champion boxer of the town. There was none who dared challenge young Eisenhower's prowess.

But one day, there came to town another young man. He gave his name as Frankie Brown. Brown bore the reputation of a professional boxer, and he soon learned of the ambitious young Eisenhower. A match was arranged between the two young athletes. No one was ever able to tell who won the honors, but both fought so well that before the bout was over, the two were fast friends.

They retired to a restaurant following the affair, and there they discussed plans for their future. Eisenhower desired to go to college, but Brown wanted to pursue boxing as a professional career. Eisenhower sought to persuade Brown first to acquire the higher schooling. In the wee hours of the night, the two emerged, both determined to go to college.[2]

Frankie Brown entered Notre Dame—as Knute Kenneth Rockne. The determination that led him to follow Dwight Eisenhower's advice also stood him in hand in becoming the noted and beloved football coach of Notre Dame.

In a fateful hour on March 31, 1931, the airplane in which Knute Rockne traveled to see his old friend in Kansas crashed to earth, crushing a life that had matched the determination, friendship, and prowess of an Eisenhower.

Once, while sitting in a restaurant, the late Henry Ford was asked: "Who is your best friend?"

Ford thought for a moment, then took out his pencil and wrote in large letters on the tablecloth: "My best friend is the one who brings out the best in me."[3]

Rockne and Eisenhower's friendship exemplified this belief. They challenged each other, encouraged each other to raise the bar on their personal expectations, and built a relationship around mutual respect. That combination inspired Knute Rockne and Dwight Eisenhower to reach for their potential.

It's enjoyable to have friends who make us laugh. I cherish friends who offer sincere advice. Friends who want to understand what's important to me are so valuable. I respect friends who genuinely celebrate my successes and encourage me through my failures. I don't want to leave out friends who help me maintain my child-like, fun spirit, but the friend who challenges me to be all God intended can't be replaced. Everybody needs a friend like that.

The easiest kind of relationship for me is with ten thousand people. The hardest is with one.

—Joan Baez[4]

Chapter 18

DEVELOP THE ABILITY
TO ASK QUESTIONS

He who asks a question is a fool for five minutes; he who does
not ask a question remains a fool forever.

—Chinese Proverb[1]

ISIDOR ISAAC RABI, WINNER OF the 1994 Nobel Prize in Physics,
relates the following memory of his childhood.

My mother made me a scientist without ever intending to.
Every other Jewish mother in Brooklyn would ask her child
after school, "So? Did you learn anything today?" But not my
mother. "Izzy," she would say, "did you ask a good question
today?" That difference—asking good questions—made me
become a scientist.[2]

It's not popular to ask questions. Instead, we are rewarded when we have the answer, can share a valuable insight, or have something to say that others haven't thought of. You're supposed to look smart in our society. That's a measuring stick for success—or is it?

When I ask you to explain something, my knowledge increases. Your's doesn't. You answered the question, so I received the gift of information. All you did is regurgitate what you already knew. How boring is that? You've learned nothing.

An old Danish proverb asserts, "People who are afraid of asking are ashamed of learning."[3] I'm not sure I was ashamed of learning, but I developed a fear of asking questions in the seventh grade. That habit followed me well into my adult life. I desperately hoped I would not be put in situations where I would not have the right answer or be expected to comment on a subject about which I had minimal knowledge.

Today, I realize the fundamental way for me to learn is by asking questions, not by having the right answers. It doesn't bother me anymore to sit in a meeting and have to say, "I don't know," or, "I'm not sure I understand your point; tell me more."

People who sit in meetings, seminars, or church services and say "Uh-huh" and nod their heads in agreement but walk out wondering what people were talking about are stripping their lives of valuable learning opportunities.

The more I know, the less I really know, but I have come to one conclusion. The world isn't necessarily divided into winners and losers, strong and weak, successes and failures. Look around at the people you know. They can probably be categorized into learners and nonlearners, question-askers and advice-givers, and those who empty their minds and those who fill their minds. The person who thinks he has all the answers isn't up to date on the present questions.

Swallow your pride. Don't listen to that little voice inside telling you that you must know everything or that you already do. Great learners are inquisitive and unaffected by a self-conscious fear of appearing unlearned. They remain motivated to expand their personal horizons, and they realize questions are creative acts of intelligence.

Be smart—ask questions.

> The best cure for a sluggish mind is to disturb its routine.
> —William H. Danforth[4]

Chapter 19

ARE YOU FILLING PEOPLE UP
OR SUCKING THEM DRY?

To do something, however small, to make others happier and
better is the highest ambition, the most elevating hope, which
can inspire a human being.

—John Lubbock[1]

SUCCESS AND FULFILLMENT IN LIFE are in direct proportion
to the investment we make in people. If someone spent the
whole day with you, how would they feel at the end of the day—
filled up or sucked dry? Are you the kind of person who searches for
ways to inject hope, encouragement, and goodwill into others, or do
you extract those necessities from others in your daily interaction?

The good news is that no one needs to live a minute longer
extracting life out of people. We can all increase our building, filling,
and replenishing habits. By doing so, we make it possible for people
to like themselves and their lives better when they are with us.

You want that, don't you? Not sure how? Consider the following
practical actions to put on your daily relationship agenda.

Remember the basics. In 1860, the Lady Elgin collided with a lumber barge on a stormy night and sank, leaving three hundred ninety-three people stranded in the waters of Lake Michigan. Two hundred seventy-nine of these people drowned. A young college student named Edward Spencer plunged into the water again and again to rescue people. After he had pulled seventeen people from the freezing water, he was overcome with exhaustion and collapsed, never to stand again. For the remainder of his life, Spencer was confined to a wheelchair. Some years later, it was noted that not one of the seventeen persons he saved ever came to thank him.[2]

How could seventeen, who had their lives spared by this young man, fail to show their gratitude? Before we judge them too harshly, it might be worth our time to evaluate our consistency in remembering life's basic manners. Smile. Say "please" and "thank you." Use people's first names when visiting with them. Greet people with a hearty "hello" or "good morning." Show interest in your coworkers' welfare. Maintain a positive, optimistic outlook on matters many people tend to frown at. Think about how others feel. Be an advocate of dignity and respect for all people.

The value of these basics is too often overlooked, taken for granted, or missed completely. These simple actions communicate the caring and compassionate attitudes that encouragers possess. Review the list again. Find ways to frequently do the little acts of kindness that produce big dividends.

Honk an encouraging message. Have you ever noticed how some friendships, marriages, and parent-child relationships are vibrant and growing while others seem to be plagued with discouragement? It may be a difference in attitude. If people build up and encourage one another, the whole atmosphere is refreshing. But critical, negative spirits breed tension and conflict.

Bruce Larson, in his book *Wind & Fire,* illustrates the power of encouragement. Writing about sand hill cranes, he wrote, "These large birds, who fly great distances across continents, have three remarkable qualities. First, they rotate leadership. No one bird stays out in front all the time. Second, they choose leaders who can handle turbulence. And then [this is my favorite], all during the time one bird is leading, the rest are honking their affirmation."[3]

Conduct an attitude check. Are you critical of people, situations, and life in general? Do you complain about the job someone else is doing or should have done? Do you have a negative spirit? If so, work to become a positive "honking" friend, spouse, parent, or coworker. Negative sourpusses are energy suckers. Positive horn honkers inspire others to fly farther and higher.

Isn't it amazing how the unique habits of a sand hill crane are applicable to us? When people consistently build up and encourage, the whole atmosphere of their relationships is nurturing. People feel safe. They are comfortable taking risks. They experience healthier feelings about themselves. Virginia Arcastle said, "When people are made to feel secure, important, and appreciated, it will no longer be necessary for them to whittle down others in order to seem bigger in comparison."[4]

Check your interactions. What kind of messages have you been honking lately? Any affirmation?

Believe in people. Dale Carnegie said, "Tell your child, your husband, or your employee that he or she is stupid or dumb at a certain thing, has no gift for it, and is doing it all wrong, and you have destroyed almost every incentive to try to improve. But use the opposite technique—be liberal with your encouragement, make the thing seem easy to do; let the other person know that you have faith in his ability to do it, that he has an undeveloped flair for it—and he will practice until the dawn comes in the window in order to excel."[5]

According to a selection in the March 1992 *Homemade*, a young man in London wanted to be a writer, but the cards seemed stacked against him. He had only four years of school, and his father was in jail because he couldn't pay his debts. Just to survive the pain of hunger, he got a job pasting labels on bottles in a rat-infested warehouse. He slept in an attic with two other boys from the slums. With such little confidence in himself and in his ability to write, he secretly slipped out in the middle of the night to mail his first manuscript so nobody would laugh at his dream. That manuscript, along with countless others, was rejected. Finally, one story was accepted. He wasn't paid anything, but the editor praised him for his writing. That one little compliment caused him to wander aimlessly through the streets with tears rolling down his cheeks. The compliment inspired him to continue and improve. It also led to a brilliant career for Charles Dickens.[6]

Donald Laird said, "Always help people increase their own self-esteem. Develop your skill in making other people feel important. There is hardly a higher compliment you can pay an individual than helping him be useful and to find satisfaction from his usefulness."[7]

Expressing your belief and faith in people can provide the inspiration for someone to pursue their dreams. Find the seed of achievement waiting for your nourishment. Help people believe in themselves more than they believe in themselves, and watch them blossom.

Express your love. I fear too many of us might be represented by the guy who exclaimed to his wife, "Honey, when I think about how much I love you, I can hardly keep from telling you."

Telling someone how much they mean to you seems like a basic relationship action—and it should be. But it's not. We may want to tell others how much they mean to us, but we don't. We want to hear words of love and affection and are disappointed at how infrequent those messages touch our ears. By our very nature, our hearts respond to a message of love.

In his book *In the Arena,* former President Richard Nixon reflected on the depression he experienced following his resignation from the presidency and then undergoing surgery. At the depths of his discouragement, he told his wife, Pat, that he just wanted to die.

At Mr. Nixon's lowest point, a nurse entered the room, pulled open the drapes, and pointed to a small airplane flying back and forth. The plane was pulling a banner which read: God Loves You, And So Do We. Ruth Graham, evangelist Billy Graham's wife, had arranged for the plane to fly by the hospital. That's when Nixon experienced a turning point. Seeing that expression of love gave him the courage and desire to keep going and recover.[8]

Somebody once said, "Appreciating others without telling them is like winking at someone in the dark; you know what you're doing, but nobody else does."

Don't just think about expressing your love and appreciation for those you care about. Take the initiative. Don't wait for the other person; the two of you could wait a long time. Never assume people know how you feel about them. Give someone close to you a hug, pat them on the back, and say, "I love you," or "You mean a lot to me," or "I care about you."

It feels good.

Someone might say, "I'm not into this 'touchy-feely' stuff. I'm uncomfortable giving hugs or verbal praise." If you are saying amen to that, here's another option: write a letter or send a note to brighten someone's day. Who could benefit from a note of appreciation, a word of concern, or a card complimenting them for a job well done? Don't let the impulse slip by without taking action. Tread yourself a well-worn path to the mailbox.

Uphold people's self-esteem. I like Henry Ward Beecher's observation that, "There are persons so radiant, so genial, so kind, so pleasure-bearing, that you instinctively feel good in their presence that they do you good, whose coming into a room is like bringing a lamp there."[9]

I had the privilege of working several years as a volunteer with junior high youth in a basketball program. It would be self-gratifying to say I was always the type of person Beecher described, but I wasn't. I did learn, however, that when I built up a young person's self-esteem, they were open to instruction.

Imagine twelve-year-old Laurie struggling to get the little round ball through the round cylinder. She's zero for ten, and you approach her saying, "Laurie, I like the way you put everything into your shot. I think you're going to make a good basketball player."

Laurie beams. She is receptive and eager to learn more. Laurie is all ears when you add, "Laurie, you tend to throw your elbow out and shoot off your palms. Let me show you the proper shooting method."

Sounds simple, doesn't it? The beauty is that upholding a person's self-esteem is simple if our motives are right. Rather than being intent on correction, let your instruction be grounded in affirmation.

The following illustration from "Our Daily Bread" puts the finishing touches on the importance of upholding self-esteem.

Benjamin West was just trying to be a good babysitter for his little sister, Sally. While his mother was out, Benjamin found some bottles of colored ink and proceeded to paint Sally's portrait. By the time Mrs. West returned, ink blots stained the table, chairs, and floor. Benjamin's mother surveyed the mess without a word until she saw the picture. Picking it up she exclaimed, "Why, it's Sally!" And she bent down and kissed her son.

In 1763, when Benjamin was twenty-five years old, he was selected as history painter to England's King George III. He became one of the most celebrated artists of his day. Commenting on his start as an artist, he said, "My mother's kiss made me a painter."[10] Her encouragement did far more than a rebuke would have done.

Each of us yearns for someone to fill us, build us, and lift us up. We encounter plenty of people along the way intent on letting us know where we've failed, fallen short of expectations, or what areas of our lives are less than perfect. These energy suckers are a dime a dozen. We need people who make us feel valued and worthwhile just as we are.

Remember the basics: honk encouraging words, believe in people more than they believe in themselves, freely express your love, and uphold people's self-esteem.

Make it possible for people to say, "I like myself better when I'm with you."

Do not do unto others as you expect they should do unto you.
Their tastes may not be the same.

—George Bernard Shaw[11]

Chapter 20

IF YOU AIN'T THE LEAD HORSE, WATCH YOUR STEP

Once you say you are going to settle for second, that's what happens to you in life.

—John F. Kennedy[1]

I NEVER THOUGHT OUR FAMILY WOULD be the type to choose a summer vacation at a ranch. However, the accidental purchase at a benefit auction of a week's stay left us little option.

The experience was surprisingly delightful—one activity especially. My daughter and I decided to take advantage of the ranch's two-hour horse trail ride. As we chose our horses, my daughter was immediately attracted to a smaller, brown-and-white spotted horse. By the time I got her situated, my choices were slim. I ended up with notably the oldest horse in the herd.

A few minutes into the trail ride (we were just outside the corral), my daughter's spunky horse began acting up a bit and performing a few acrobatic maneuvers. The trail ride leaders came immediately to assist and momentarily calm the anxious horse. My daughter quickly pointed me out as her dad, and the leaders asked if I would take up the rear with my daughter's horse directly in front of me. They assured me that it was a position the spotted horse enjoyed and that no further antics were anticipated.

I was a bit concerned riding through the mountains that my daughter could be quickly thrown from her horse, so I kept my eyes attached to the rear of her horse. For two and a half hours I enjoyed very little sight-seeing but instead learned plenty about a horse's back-half activities.

We survived the ride. My daughter had a great time and became buddy-buddy with the horse she affectionately named "Brown Sugar." But there was more to the trail ride for me than stiff legs, saddle sores, and smelling like a livestock sale barn. I came to a few conclusions.

If you ain't the lead horse, the view never changes. Riding in the rear of the pack—intently focused on my daughter's horse and with a limited view of the sights ahead—inhibited my ability to enjoy the ride.

Helen Keller was once asked what would be worse than being blind. She quickly replied, "To have sight and no vision."[2] People who are continually focused on the immediate fail to see what could be. Shortsighted living leaves people doing the same things, thinking the same thoughts, controlled by the same habits, and getting the same results. Boring!

Catapult your position forward in the pack by overcoming your addiction to old methodologies. Grasp a vision of something new and beyond your mental boundaries. See possibilities you've been blinded to by limited vision. Shift gears by adopting new thoughts and actions.

If you ain't the lead horse, watch your step. I learned quickly that the worst part of being in the rear of the pack is trying to avoid stepping in what the other horses leave behind.

Complacency must be eliminated to overcome the satisfaction of settling for second best, stuck with what's left over. If you don't get what you want, it is a sign that you've probably destined yourself to accepting whatever comes your way rather than carefully calculating the results you desire. Don't shortchange yourself! Program your life to step over the obstacles created by other people, circumstances, or your present condition. Position yourself to pioneer uncharted terrain. It sure beats constantly avoiding what others leave behind.

Staying on the well-worn path offers little adventure. Trail-ride horses are conditioned to follow the pack. Their mission is to remain on the trail they have traveled hundreds of times. People are no different. We develop rut-driven lifestyles. No fresh vision. No new land. No risks. This is what Phillips Brooks was referring to when he said, "Sad is the day for any man when he becomes absolutely satisfied with the life that he is living, the thoughts he is thinking and the deeds he is doing; until there ceases to be forever beating at the door of his soul a desire to do something larger which he seeks and knows he was meant and intended to do."[3]

If you ain't the lead horse, think about Frederic Flach's comment in his book *Choices*. "Most people can look back over the years and identify a time and place at which their lives changed significantly. Whether by accident or design, these are the moments when because of a readiness within us and a collaboration with events occurring around us, we are forced to seriously reappraise ourselves and the conditions under which we live to make certain choices that will affect the rest of our lives."[4]

Make that choice today. You can make a difference in the enjoyment you experience on life's trail ride.

> Conformity is the jailer of freedom and the enemy of growth.
> —John F. Kennedy[5]

Section Six

ENCOURAGEMENT

Chapter 21

OFFER A SHOULDER TO LEAN ON

Few things in the world are more powerful than a positive push. A smile. A word of optimism and hope. A "you can do it" when things are tough.

—Richard M. DeVos[1]

THE 1992 OLYMPICS IN BARCELONA, Spain, provided spectators with a multitude of great moments. Reruns of one track and field event live in my memory.

Britain's Derek Redmond had a lifelong dream of winning a gold medal in the 400-meter race. His chances of achieving that dream increased when the gun sounded to begin the semifinals in Barcelona. Redmond was running a great race, and the finish line was clearly in sight as he rounded the turn in the backstretch. Then disaster struck. A sharp pain shot up the back of his leg. He fell face first onto the track with a torn right hamstring.

Sports Illustrated provided this account of the events that followed:

As the medical attendants were approaching, Redmond fought to his feet. "It was animal instinct," he would say later. He set out hopping, in a crazed attempt to finish the race. When he reached the stretch, a large man in a T-shirt came out of the stands, hurled aside a security guard and ran to Redmond, embracing him. It was Jim Redmond, Derek's father. "You don't have to do this," he told his weeping son. "Yes, I do," said Derek. "Well, then," said Jim, "We're going to finish this together."

And they did. Fighting off security men, the son's head sometimes buried in his father's shoulder, they stayed in Derek's lane all the way to the end, as the crowd gaped, then rose and howled and wept.[2]

What a dramatic sight! Derek Redmond failed to capture a gold medal, but he left Barcelona with an incredible memory of a father who left the crowd to share his son's pain. Together, they limped to the finish.

What does this say to us? There isn't a person alive who hasn't experienced the disappointment of unmet expectations. Things don't always go as planned in the pursuit of our dreams. Unexpected obstacles, unplanned events, or the onset of circumstances beyond our control can burst our bubbles. It is amazing how quickly our hopes can vanish followed by the pangs of failure, embarrassment, and discouragement.

A word of encouragement during a failure is worth more than a whole load of praise after a success. Orison Swett Marden said, "There is no medicine like hope, no incentive so great, and no tonics so powerful as expectation of something better tomorrow."[3] You can be the distributor of hope that propels someone past the present burden and into future possibilities.

Understanding how quickly momentum can be brought to an abrupt halt increases our sensitivity to how others feel when disappointments sabotage their dreams. It's then that people need someone who cares enough about them to come out of the crowd and onto the track. Let them know you are there for them. Offer a shoulder to lean on to help carry them through the pain. They may not attain the level of success they desired, but they'll never forget the person who lifted them up when they felt let down.

> The worst part of success is trying to find someone who is happy for you.
>
> —Bette Midler[4]

Chapter 22

HOW GOOD CAN PEOPLE BE?

You can't make the other fellow feel important in your presence if you secretly feel that he is a nobody.

—Les Giblin[1]

I READ ABOUT A YOUNG FOOTBALL coach at Louisiana State University who knew how to capitalize on high expectations. Paul Dietzel's 1958 football team was picked to finish near the bottom of the Southeastern Conference. Of his top thirty players, none weighed over 210 pounds. Their abilities were far from impressive. Dietzel eliminated the customary first, second, and third team concept. Instead, he broke his squad into three units and named them the White Team, Go Team, and Chinese Bandits. The Chinese Bandit squad would customarily be known as benchwarmers. However, Dietzel convinced them they were defensive specialists and challenged them to live up to their name.

Throughout the season, the Chinese Bandits were called upon to display their tough and aggressive defensive tactics that frequently spelled the difference between winning and losing. LSU defied all odds that year by going undefeated and being named the number one team in both the Associated Press and United Press polls.[2]

The 1958 LSU football team wasn't technically very good, but Dietzel never let them know it. He wasn't like the football coach who told his team, "We are undefeated and untied. Nobody has scored on us. Enjoy it because we now have to play our first game." Dietzel instilled a belief in his players that they could succeed, and that belief produced the power to live up to his expectations.

How good would you be if you didn't know how good you were? How good would your team be if they didn't know how good they were? How good could those around you become if you raised your expectations of them?

Create high expectations for people, and let them know you believe in them more than they believe in themselves. People succeed if someone they respect thinks they can.

> Keep away from people who try to belittle your ambitions. Small people always do that, but the really great make you feel that you, too, can become great.
>
> —Mark Twain[3]

Chapter 23

REDUCING THE STING
OF CRITICISM

A successful man is one who can lay a firm foundation with the
bricks that others throw at him.

—David Brinkley[1]

ACE IT, SOME PEOPLE HAVE photographic memories. They
remember all the negatives about the people around them.
You have probably encountered such a person and scrambled to avoid his crushing blows. Although it's true that criticism
won't kill you, its sting can have a lasting impact.

Charles Spurgeon said, "Insults are like bad coins; we cannot help
their being offered us, but we need not take them."[2] Nice words, but
easier said than done. Criticism seems to immediately cut its way to
our emotional center. It leaves scars.

We do have a choice in how we deal with the insults we encounter.
We must realize that no matter how small or large the issue might
be, our reactions can make it worse or better. When I am criticized,
I have a tendency to overreact and become defensive. I dwell on the
comment, running it through my mind over and over, attempting

to justify my actions or prove mentally how wrong the other person was. Incredible energy is wasted in this spiraling unproductive activity.

The next time you find yourself in the path of critical bricks hurled your way, learn to desensitize the impact of accusations rather than stand defenseless.

1. Consider the source. Normally it is the person who can't dance who complains about the unevenness of the floor. Likewise, people who criticize other people are frequently hurting themselves. Out of their frustration with life, they find someone else to blame. Don't take their criticism personally.

While driving along a desolate highway on a hot summer afternoon, I noticed vultures soaring high overhead, swooping down, then rising up again. Their motives were undoubtedly selfish. I watched a small group of them tear apart and devour the remains of a small animal on the side of the road. That's their lifestyle—continually on the lookout for some creature they can take advantage of. Such is often the source of criticism. Critical people tend to look for unsuspecting, vulnerable victims they can tear apart and devour. Consider the source before deciding to take seriously what has been said.

2. Smile. Have you ever tried arguing with someone who is smiling at you? If you want to disarm an attacker, take a deep breath, smile, and say, "Thank you." O. A. Bautista said, "One of the surest marks of good character is a person's ability to accept criticism without malice to the one who gives it."[3] I might add that it is of equal character to neutralize criticism before it damages you or the relationship. I'm not suggesting this is easy, but you will find it helpful in keeping critical comments in perspective.

Along with your smile, keep your sense of humor. Humor is a marvelous tool for neutralizing the sting of criticism and disapproval. It will divert your attention and diminish the affects.

I love the story of the lady who took her overworked husband to the family physician for a checkup. The physician took the wife aside and whispered: "I don't like the way your husband looks."

"I don't either," she replied, "but he's always been a good provider."

3. Expect it but don't accept it. Epictetus provided us an ideal approach to dealing with all those people with photographic memories. "If someone criticizes you, agree at once. Mention that if only the other person knew you well, there would be more to criticize than that."[4] Arguing with one who criticizes is a no-win battle, so Epictetus believed the best way to silence your critic and not waste energy was to agree with him and get on with life.

Someone once indicated there were only two critical people in the whole world—they just move around a lot and seem to pull down the masses with their cynicism. "Nothing takes a greater toll on us than to be around a pessimist—a person always finding fault and criticizing others," said Cavett Robert. "We've all seen the type. He has mental B.O. He's a one-man grievance committee, always in session."[5] Actually, criticism has become a national pastime. Sooner or later you will be the target of someone's mental B.O. Not everything everybody says about you is true. It is important that you objectively weigh the value of their comments. Learn what you can from the criticism. If they are right, work toward making changes. If they are wrong, don't spend another moment focused on the accusations.

3. Don't take it personally. Abraham Lincoln would never have achieved all he did if he had not learned to duck or build on the massive criticism he encountered. His insight is worth your consideration. "If I were to try to read, much less to answer, all the attacks made on me, this shop might as well be closed for any other business," Lincoln said. "I do the very best I know how—the very best I can; and I mean to keep doing so until the end. If the end brings me out all right, then what is said against me won't matter. If the end brings me out wrong, then ten angels swearing I was right would make no difference."[6]

Colonel George Washington Goethals faced enormous opposition as the supervisor responsible for building the Panama Canal.

Not only did his builders face incredible challenges with geography, climate, and disease, but people back home predicted they would never complete the "impossible task." The great engineer kept the faith and was resolute in steadily moving forward to complete the project without responding to his opposition.

At one point a frustrated coworker asked, "Aren't you going to answer your critics?" "In time," Goethals replied. "How?" the man asked. The colonel smiled and said, "With the canal!" That answer materialized on August 15, 1914, when the canal opened to traffic for the first time.[7]

Pressing forward. Not getting caught up in verbal warfare. Producing results. Those are often the best ways to counteract ridicule. Expect it. Don't accept it. Press on.

4. Ponder the benefits. When the legendary Knute Rockne was head football coach at Notre Dame, a column appeared in the school paper with no indication as to who wrote it, other than the signature "Old Bearskin." The columnist picked apart each player, pointing out their individual weaknesses and lambasting their shortcomings and inept performances.

Word spread quickly across campus. Players complained to Rockne that they were being unfairly criticized. Rockne would empathize with their position and encourage them to get out on the field and prove their critics wrong.

The writer of that column was never identified—that is, until after Rockne died. And guess what? "Old Bearskin" was actually the players' best friend and their coach. Yes, Rockne penned the article. He was aware of what happened to football legends whose success on the field went to their heads. As "Old Bearskin," his criticisms were an attempt to help them avoid the pitfalls of pride and strive continually to achieve new levels of performance.

As unfair as criticism might be, it can also be a helpful reminder to avoid the pitfalls of success. Corrie ten Boom believes, "Our critics are the unpaid guardians of our souls."[8] That may be a bit difficult to swallow, but with an open mind, the perceptions of others can actually assist us in keeping our talents fine-tuned. The master retailer Marshall Field maintained a healthy attitude about criticism. He said, "Those who enter to buy support me. Those who come to flatter please me. Those who complain teach me how I may please others so that more will come. Only those hurt me who are displeased but do not complain. They refuse me permission to correct my errors and thus improve my service."[9]

I had the unfortunate experience of going to the doctor to determine the source of my severe stomach pain. As I lay on the examination table he began to poke, prod, and push in various areas all the while asking, "Does this hurt? How about this?" It was an unpleasant experience.

When I flinched with pain each time he pressed a certain area, it was evident that he was either pressing too hard without the right sensitivity or it was a problem area. In my case, additional tests were required, resulting in the diagnosis of an infection and the need for treatment.

So it is with criticism. Crying out with discomfort might be an indication that there is need for additional attention. Maybe someone is just pushing a hot button and is not as sensitive as he should be. You can't control the critical people in your life, but what you do with criticism is your decision.

> I can please only one person per day. Today is not your day. Tomorrow isn't looking good either.
> —Dilbert's Words of Wisdom[10]

Chapter 24

HELPING PEOPLE BELIEVE IN THEMSELVES

Those who believe in our ability do more than stimulate us. They create for us an atmosphere in which it becomes easier to succeed.

—John H. Spalding[1]

Yogi Berra was asked whether he thought Don Mattingly's performance in 1984 exceeded his expectations. Yogi responded, "No, but he did a lot better than I thought he would."[2]

Yogi Berra was a master of confusing messages. Yet, our message concerning what we expect of others is normally received loud and clear.

Tommy was having a difficult time in school. He was full of questions and tended to fall behind on class assignments. Tommy's teacher became frustrated with his performance and told his mother that Tommy had little chance for academic achievement or life success.

Tommy's mother believed differently. She removed Tommy from the low-expectation environment and taught him herself. She nurtured his inquisitive nature and encouraged him to use failure as a signal to find another way.

What happened? Tommy became an inventor, recording more than a thousand patents. We can thank him for the lights in our homes and countless other electronic inventions. Thomas Edison thrived on the hope created by his mother's positive expectations.[3]

Our mission in relationships should be not to impress others but to get people to believe in themselves. When we express faith, the door is opened for people to think higher of themselves. That confidence in themselves creates an environment where people feel safe to risk going beyond where they are. Every time you express positive expectations in someone, you are providing life-sustaining nutrition.

Rent the movie *Stand and Deliver*. Watch how calculus teacher Jaime Escalante worked with high school students in East Los Angeles. Keep in mind that was a part of the country where high expectations were virtually non-existent and the idea of quality education was a hopeless pursuit.

Escalante endeavored to work with his students to exceed all previous society-imposed and self-imposed limitations. He was committed to offering them an opportunity to believe in themselves and create hope for the future. His students responded.

I smiled when the Educational Testing Service voiced their skepticism about the results earned by Escalante's students. The ETS investigated the class for cheating. Ultimately, the service provider had to admit that Escalante's students had honorably achieved their scores. This great teacher challenged their minds and instilled belief in themselves.[4]

In order for you to get people to feel important, you must see their value. What I look for in people, I see. What I see, I communicate. What I communicate stimulates people to respond accordingly. What do you see in and expect of others?

The only person who behaves sensibly is my tailor. He takes my measurements anew every time he sees me, while all the rest go on with their old measurements and expect me to fit them.

—George Bernard Shaw[5]

Section Seven

UNDERSTANDING

Chapter 25

WHOSE LANGUAGE ARE YOU SPEAKING?

> If I can listen to what he can tell me, if I can understand how it seems to him, if I can see its personal meaning for him, if I can sense the emotional flavor which it has for him, then I will be releasing potent forces of change within him.
>
> —Carl Rogers[1]

D R. ROBERT SCHULLER, IN HIS book *Reach Out for New Life*, tells a story about an incident that occurred many years ago in England. The character at the heart of the story was the most famous elephant in the circus world named Bozo.

Bozo was a beautiful beast—a great big tender hunk of gentleness. Children would come to the circus and extend their chubby open palms filled with peanuts through the gate. With tender eyes and a mobile nose, the elephant would drop his trunk, pick the peanuts out of their hands, curl his trunk, and feed himself. He seemed to smile as he swallowed the gifts. Everyone loved Bozo.

Then one day something happened that changed his personality from positive to negative almost overnight. One day he almost stampeded, threatening to crush the man who was cleaning his cage. Then he began to charge the children. The circus owner knew the elephant was now dangerous and that the problem had to be faced. He came to the conclusion that he would have to exterminate this big old beast. This decision hurt him because he loved the elephant, and Bozo was the only elephant he had. Bozo had been imported from India; it would cost him thousands of pounds to replace him.

Then he got an idea. This desperate and crude man decided that he would sell tickets to view the execution of Bozo. At least he would be able to raise the money to replace him.

The story spread, tickets were sold out, and the place was jammed. There, on the appointed date, Bozo waited in his cage as three men with high-powered rifles rose to take aim at the great beast's head.

Just before the signal to shoot, a little stubby man with a brown derby hat stepped out of the crowd, walked over to the owner, and said, "Sir, this is not necessary. This is not a bad elephant." The owner said, "But it is. We must kill him before he kills someone." The little man with the derby hat said, "Sir, give me two minutes alone in his cage, and I'll prove that you are wrong. He is not a bad elephant."

The circus owner thought for a moment, wrung his hands and said, "All right. But first you must sign a note absolving me of all responsibility if you get killed."

The little man scribbled on a piece of paper the words, "I absolve you of all guilt," signed his name, folded the paper, and handed it to the circus owner. The owner opened the door to the cage. The little man threw his brown derby hat on the ground and stepped into the cage. As soon as he was inside, the door was locked behind him. The elephant raised his trunk, bellowed, and trumpeted loudly.

Before the elephant charged, the little man began talking to him, looking him straight in the eye. The people could hear the little man talking, but they couldn't understand what he was saying. It seemed as if he was speaking in an unknown tongue. The elephant still trembled, but while hearing these strange words from this little man he began to whine, cry, and wave his head back and forth. Now the stranger walked up to Bozo and began to stroke his trunk. The now gentle beast tenderly wrapped his trunk around the feet of the little man, lifted him up, carried him around his cage and cautiously put him back down at the door. Everyone applauded.

As he walked out of the cage, the little man said to the keeper, "You see? He is a good elephant. His only problem is that he is an Indian elephant, and he only understands Hindustani. He was homesick for someone who could understand him. I suggest, sir, that you find someone in London who speaks Hindustani, and have him come in and just talk to the elephant. You'll have no problems."

As the man picked up his derby and walked away, the circus owner looked at the note and read the signature of the man who had signed it. The man with the little brown derby was Rudyard Kipling.[2]

Dr. Schuller said, "People also become frustrated, angry, and defeated when no one understands them."[3] Could it be that the person you are having a difficult time with just needs someone to understand his situation, to speak his language?

John Luther believed, "Natural talent, intelligence, a wonderful education—none of these guarantees success. Something else is needed: The sensitivity to understand what other people want and the willingness to give it to them."[4]

> One learns people through the heart, not the eyes or the intellect.
>
> —Mark Twain[5]

Chapter 26

THE REASONS PEOPLE DO THINGS

If you pick up a starving dog and make him prosperous, he will not bite you. This is the principal difference between a man and a dog.

—Mark Twain[1]

ITHINK MARK TWAIN WAS HAVING a bad day when he made that statement. Although there is good reason for the common theory that a dog is man's best friend, even a dog can become disillusioned if the relationship is a one-way affair. Let me explain what I mean.

Ralph Waldo Emerson was a great historian, poet, and philosopher, but he didn't know much about getting a stubborn calf through a barn door. One day, Emerson and his son were involved in such a challenge. Can't you just see the son with his arms around the calf's neck and Emerson in the rear braced to push with all his might? As they pushed and pulled repeatedly, the calf braced itself by locking her knees and digging her feet into the ground, determined not to comply.

Drenched with sweat, full of bovine smell, and frustrated to the point of exasperation, Emerson stood helpless over the calf. An Irish servant girl, who had observed the comical pursuit, approached Emerson and asked if she could be of assistance. She walked around to the front of the calf, thrust her finger into the calf's mouth, and the calf peacefully followed the girl into the barn.[2]

Bob Conklin, in *How to Get People to Do Things,* said, "People are like that calf. You can poke them, prod them, push them, and they don't move. But give them a good reason—one of their reasons, a way in which they will benefit—and they will follow gently along. People will do things for *their* reasons. Not *your* reasons. And those reasons are emotional, aroused by the way they feel."[3]

People do things for their reasons—not your reasons. This is one of the greatest and yet simplest principles of human relations. People do things because they want to, not because you want them to. As Lord Chesterfield advised, "If you will please people, you must please them in their own way."[4]

Once we understand that relationships evolve around people's needs and expectations, it's more natural to create an environment where mutual warmth and love exist.

What do people need? What are the reasons people do things? What are the qualities we display that cause people to want to pursue and maintain a relationship with us?

Don't make this too philosophical or difficult. In many ways, Anthony Robbins's comment that, "When people are like each other, they tend to like each other"[5] provides a hint to the answers we're looking for. The same things that cause you to be drawn to someone, often times open the door for others to feel comfortable with you.

Make a list of the qualities, actions, and attitudes of people you enjoy being around. Endeavor to sharpen and refine those attributes in your life. There is no shortcut to nourishing relationships, but understanding what people need is the shortest connection between where you are and where you want your relationships to be.

To counter Mark Twain's cynical comparison between people and dogs, perhaps we should consider that oftentimes we give more thought and energy to what our dog wants and likes than we do our spouse, children, and friends.

> Needing someone is like needing a parachute. If he isn't there the first time you need him, chances are you won't be needing him again.
>
> —Dilbert's Words of Wisdom[6]

Chapter 27

PUTTING YOURSELF IN THEIR WORLD

To love you as I love myself is to seek to hear you as I want to be heard and understand you as I long to be understood.

—David Augsburger[1]

MY DAUGHTER BECAME FRUSTRATED A few weeks into her freshman year of high school. Normally a happy, vivacious, young lady, she felt overwhelmed by the pressures of school, conflict with friends, teacher expectations, and the time demands of extra-curricular activities. As Katy told me her traumatic experiences, I tried to console her by telling her everything would be okay and that she need not be distressed by these minor difficulties.

"That's easy for you to say, Dad," she responded. "You have all your problems over with."

From a teenager's perspective, adults are all through with their problems and life is one continuous party. Even more important, I think Katy was trying to tell me she could use a little empathy. She wanted me to understand what it feels like to be a freshman. I gave my daughter sound, practical, and realistic advice when all she really wanted was an understanding heart. This could have been a magical father-daughter moment. Instead, it was just another conversation.

Poet Shel Silverstein wrote a heart-touching verse entitled, "The Little Boy and the Old Man." In it is portrayed a young boy talking to an elderly gentleman.

> Said the little boy, "Sometimes I drop my spoon."
> Said the old man, "I do that too."
> The little boy whispered, "I wet my pants."
> "I do that too," laughed the little old man.
> Said the little boy, "I often cry."
> The old man nodded, "So do I."
> "But worst of all," said the boy, "it seems
> Grown-ups don't pay attention to me."
> And he felt the warmth of a wrinkled old hand.
> "I know what you mean," said the little old man.[2]

Most people think they see the world as it is. Unfortunately, we really see the world as we are.

I saw my daughter's difficulties through the eyes of a grown-up, not a high school freshman. The little boy saw the world through his eyes, which he learned were much like the eyes of the old man. In a world obsessed with "me" there is a tremendous opportunity to touch people's lives by focusing on what's important to them.

A common obstacle to understanding another person is the limiting belief that his or her world mirrors mine.

I know that doesn't sound too profound, but the significance of that statement is an entryway to people's hearts. To realize that others don't necessarily think like me, act like me, feel like I feel, or respond to every situation as I would respond prepares me to gain valuable insights that might otherwise have been overlooked.

The ability to truly understand other people is a valuable asset. It involves opening your mind and heart with an insatiable desire to help people feel understood. A sincere attempt is made in every conversation to think how others think and feel what others are feeling. If every conversation began and evolved around this intent, I wonder how many conflicts could be avoided.

Are your daily conversations motivated by a desire to get people to understand you, or are you committed in every conversation to put yourself in the other person's world? See their world, experiences, hopes, fears, and dreams as they see them. The benefits are immeasurable, because for every person we sincerely seek to understand, there will be someone who wants to do the same for us.

Make it possible for someone today to say, "When I'm with you, I feel understood."

> Sometimes you can defuse a difficult situation simply by being willing to understand the other person. Often all that people need is to know that someone else cares about how they feel and is attempting to understand their position.
>
> —Brian Tracy[3]

Chapter 28

COULD YOU JUST LISTEN?

> Most of the successful people I've known are ones who do more
> listening than talking. If you choose your company carefully,
> it's worth listening to what they have to say. You don't have to
> blow out the other fellow's light to let your own shine.
>
> —Bernard M. Baruch[1]

IT HAPPENS ABOUT ONCE A week. My wife and I have a nice conversation about a favorite topic, or she will fill me in on the details of an upcoming event. A little while later, I ask a question that she already addressed in our conversation. She then looks at me and says, "You never listen to me." Ouch. I do listen, I think, but for some reason a portion of the information just seems to leak from my memory. Although I think I know how to listen, my actions often prove different.

John Maxwell tells a delightful story about an eighty-nine-year-old woman with hearing problems who visited her doctor. After examining her, the doctor said, "We now have a procedure that can correct your hearing problem. When would you like to schedule the operation?"

"There won't be any operation because I don't want my hearing corrected," said the woman. "I'm eighty-nine years old, and I've heard enough!"[2]

There are times, at any age, when we might think, "I've heard enough, and I don't care to listen anymore." Karl Menninger believes, "The friends who listen to us are the ones we move toward, and we want to sit in their radius."[3] If a relationship is important to us, it is wise to remember that the difference between someone feeling comfortable with us or avoiding us is often our willingness to listen.

The following poem reveals the feelings of someone who badly wants to be heard.

> When I ask you to listen to me
> and you start giving me advice,
> you have not done what I asked.
>
> When I ask you to listen to me
> and you tell me I shouldn't feel that way,
> you are trampling on my feelings.
>
> When I ask you to listen to me
> and you feel you have to do something to solve my problem,
> you have failed me, strange as that may seem.
>
> Listen! All I asked was that you listen,
> not talk to or do—just hear me.
>
> Advice is cheap—10 cents will get you both Dear Abby
> and Billy Graham in the same newspaper.
>
> I can do that for myself; I'm not helpless—,
> maybe discouraged and faltering, but not helpless.
>
> When you do something for me that I can and need to do
> for myself, you contribute to my fear and weakness.

But, when you accept as a simple fact that I do feel what I feel,
no matter how irrational,
then I can quit trying to convince you
and can get get about the business of understanding what's behind
this irrational feeling.

And when that's clear, the answers are obvious
and I don't need advice.
Irrational feelings make sense when we understand.

Perhaps that's why prayer works, sometimes, for some people
because God is mute and He doesn't give advice or try to fix
    things.
"They" just listen and let you work it out for yourself.

So, please listen and just hear me.
And, if you want to talk, wait a minute for your turn—
and I'll listen to you.

                                        —Anonymous[4]

This unknown writer was expressing a frustration experienced every day by a multitude of people. From the corporate office to the school playground, from the hospital room to the bedroom, and from the subway to the carpool, you will find people who genuinely feel that no one is interested in their lives. Paul Tournier addressed this universal need. "It is impossible," he said, "to over-emphasize the immense need humans have to be really listened to, to be taken seriously, to be understood. No one can develop freely in this world and find their life full, without feeling understood by at least one person… Listen to all the conversations of our world, between nations as well as between couples. They are for the most part, dialogues of the deaf."[5]

Studies indicate that we spend 30 percent of a normal business day speaking, 16 percent reading, 9 percent writing, and 45 percent—the majority of our time—listening. Yet, very few people have studied or mastered listening techniques even though close to half of our day is spent in such activity.[6]

An unofficial listening study offers this perspective: "We hear half of what is being said, listen to half of what we hear, understand half of it, believe half of that, and remember only half of that." If you translate those assumptions into an eight-hour work day, it means that:

- You spend half your day—about four hours—in listening activities.
- You hear about two hours' worth of what is said.
- You actually listen to an hour of it.
- You understand only thirty minutes of that hour.
- You believe only fifteen minutes' worth.
- And you remember less than eight minutes of all that is said.[7]

Statistics indicate the importance and difficulty of listening as well as the widespread listening incompetence most people display. The world needs people who aspire to be listeners. Ironically, they not only enhance others' lives but their own as well. It is a win-win affair, and the benefits of acquiring this important skill are enjoyed throughout our lives.

> Listening, like readying, is primarily an activity of the mind, not of the ear or the eye. When the mind is not actively involved in the process, it should be called hearing, not listening.
>
> —Mortimer Adler[8]

COMMUNICATION

Chapter 29

FOR MEN ONLY

The reason you don't understand me...is because I'm talking
to you in English and you're listening in dingbat.

—Archie Bunker[1]

DR. PAUL FAULKNER BELIEVES THERE is a distinct difference in the listening ability between men and women. In
his book, *Making Things Right When Things Go Wrong*, Dr.
Faulkner suggests that women are wired for 440 volts! They have
little emotional wires sticking out from them in all directions. They
are wired for sound and two-way communication. They talk and
receive. They hook into another person's emotions and needs.

On the other hand, men are wired for 12 volts. That's all. They
have two little wires sticking out, and they're both bent. Their
speakers are usually hooked up, but their receivers are dead. So,
men have to work a lot harder to listen than women do. Men are just
wired up differently. They are like two tin cans and a waxed string,
but women are hooked up like Ma Bell.[2]

A television example from my generation let us watch how Archie
and Edith Bunker's communication difficulties probably had little

to do with one speaking English and the other communicating in "dingbat." Dr. Faulkner might suggest that Archie Bunker give some serious attention to his bent wires and dead receiver.

Now that I think about it, I'm going to put additional effort into my own 12-volt wiring system. I think I can actually improve my reception. What about you?

> Before a marriage, a man will lie awake all night thinking about something you said; after marriage, he'll fall asleep before you finish saying it.
>
> —Helen Rowland[3]

Chapter 30

MASTERING A RARE
SECRET TO SUCCESS

You ain't learnin' nothin' when you're talkin.'
> —Lyndon D. Johnson[1]

ENRY FORD SUGGESTED, "IF THERE is any one secret to success it lies in the ability to get the other person's point of view and see things from that person's angle as well as from your own."[2]

Effective listening plays a major role in our ability to understand situations from another person's perspective, thereby ensuring a mutual understanding. Henry Ford considered this ability so important that he promoted it as a secret to success. Consider these four major principles for successful listening. These practical and proven techniques will increase your impact on people dramatically.

1. Develop a willingness to listen. Your heart, not your ears, determines your listening efficiency. It has been said that "when the heart is willing it will find a thousand ways but when the heart is weak it will find a thousand excuses."[3]

How true! Listening is a desire, an attitude that wants to hear what others are saying. Dick Cavett explained why this attitude is so important. He said, "It's a rare person who wants to hear what he doesn't want to hear."[4] Developing an attitude or wanting to hear is an inside job. You can read all the books, take an array of classes, or indulge yourself with other learning sources, but the prerequisite to becoming an effective leader is developing a willingness to listen.

2. Be open-minded. "Real communication," wrote Carl Rogers, "takes place when we listen with understanding; this is, see the speaker's idea from his or her viewpoint, sense how they feel about it, and realize why they're talking about it."[5] People can be distracted from achieving this level of communication when they jump to conclusions, find fault with the message, react to emotionally charged words, or allow their prejudices to interfere with what is being said.

I rarely travel in my car without the entertainment of a motivational or educational message playing. Rarely do I argue, interrupt, or yell at my sound system. Instead, I carefully listen to the speaker's entire message, take a few written notes, and then reflect on what has been said. Even though I might not agree with everything I hear, listening selectively, paying attention only to what I agree with or blocking out topics that fail to be appealing, are not the best plans. It's critical to hear the whole message without making assumptions that block your ability to understand the other person's perspective.

The word *communication* comes from the Latin root, *communicare*, which means "to have in common." When you listen, be open-minded enough to look for common ground. This open-minded approach to listening will increase your comprehension and ability to understand the ideas and feelings being shared.

I fear that far too often our listening minds are like a seasoned consultant. An aspiring management consultant was learning the ropes from an experienced senior partner. As the novice shadowed his model, he noticed how several times a day people would dump their problems on his senior partner. The experienced consultant would make eye contact, nod, and smile warmly. Then he was on to another partner, and the same scenario would be repeated. Each day the seasoned consultant seemed to patiently listen to everyone's moans and groans.

Finally, the young man could restrain himself no longer. "I don't see how you can do it. How do you put up with listening to everyone's problems all the time and still remain so positive?"

The older consultant flashed a wry smile and said, "Who listens?"

3. Be attentive. President Abraham Lincoln said, "When I'm getting ready to reason with a man, I spend one third of my time thinking about myself and what I am going to say—and two thirds thinking about him and what he is going to say."[6] Lincoln, the master communicator, knew how important it was to be attentive to those with whom he was communicating.

Attentive listening is difficult partly because the normal person can listen at four hundred to six hundred words per minute, while the average speaking rate is two hundred to three hundred words per minute. That leaves a substantial amount of time for the mind to wander.

Maybe this explains why the normal listener retains only 50 percent of what he hears. After forty-eight hours, he retains only 25 percent; after one week, 10 percent. In addition, we listen at about a 25 percent efficiency rate, meaning that we ignore, misunderstand, or distort a majority of what we hear.

So, how can we increase our attention quotient? Become a sponge. Soak in everything the other person is saying—everything. Shut out all distractions. Remember, your mind is working at four hundred to six hundred words a minute. Therefore, to give someone your undivided attention and soak up the entire message you should do the following:

- Maintain comfortable eye contact. Don't stare.
- Don't jump to conclusions and guess what the person is going to say next.

- Refrain from interrupting. Let him or her finish.
- Be patient.
- Listen for the spoken and unspoken message.
- Don't tune people out. Keep an open mind.
- Be silent. Juggle the letters in listen, and "silent" emerges.
- Take a few notes.
- Wait to prepare your reply until the other person has finished.
- Nod, smile, agree with what is being said, and lean slightly forward. Actively participate in the conversation.
- Ask questions to clarify.
- Don't allow how people say something to distract you from what they say.
- Paraphrase what has been said. Make sure you have an accurate picture of the message.

These strategies take tremendous discipline and self-control. You can do it. Commit yourself to avoid the temptation to be distracted. You will pay people the utmost compliment by giving them your undivided attention.

4. Make people glad they talked to you. So often I assume people talk to me because they are looking for advice. More often than not, advice is the last thing they seek. People want a sympathetic ear, one that will sincerely attempt to experience what they are feeling and accept them for it. "After thirty-six years," said Ann Landers, "I realize that many people who write to me don't want advice. They just need someone who will listen."[7]

A particularly heartwarming story concerning the value of listening involves a young woman asked out on two dates. The first night she went to dinner with William E. Gladstone, the distinguished British diplomat. Upon arriving home, she was asked her opinion of the evening. "Oh," she responded, "William Gladstone is the cleverest man in England."

When her evening with the equally distinguished Benjamin Disraeli was over, the same question was posed to her. She replied thoughtfully, "Benjamin Disraeli made me feel like the cleverest woman in England."[8]

What was the difference? It has been said that really listening to someone is the highest compliment you can pay people. They will feel valued by your attention to them and what they have to say. Disraeli was known for his listening skills, and it only followed that an evening spent with him would make anyone feel important.

George and Nikki Kochler mirror the importance of affirming people through listening: "When you and I listen to another person we are conveying the thought that 'I'm interested in you as a person, and I think that what you feel is important. I respect your thoughts, even if I don't agree with them. I know that they are valid for you. I feel sure that you have a contribution to make. I'm not trying to change you or evaluate you. I just want to understand you. I think you're worth listening to, and I want you to know that I'm the kind of person that you can talk to.'"[9]

Is that the attitude that permeates your conversations? A credible way to evaluate that question is to answer this one: How important do people feel after spending time with you?

> One often reads about the art of conversation—how it's dying or what's needed to make it flourish, or how rare good ones are. But wouldn't you agree that the infinitely more valuable *rara avis* is a good listener?
>
> —Malcolm Forbes[9]

Chapter 31

UNTANGLE YOUR HORNS

> For some of the large indignities of life, the best remedy is direct action. For the small indignities, the best remedy is a Charlie Chaplin movie. The hard part is knowing the difference.
>
> —Carol Tavris[1]

I AM TOLD THAT DISPLAYED IN an old monastery near Babenhausen, Germany, are two pairs of deer antlers permanently interlocked. Apparently they were found in that position many years ago. Legend has it that the animals had been fighting fiercely, and their horns became so entangled they were unable to free themselves. As a result, both deer perished from hunger.

Imagine those entangled horns. They represent the frozen condition that conflict can create. When we are determined to have our own way, win every argument or demand our rights, we risk becoming entangled to the degree that we starve a relationship. Unresolved conflict threatens to dissolve relationships.

Heightened negative emotions can also spread to those outside the initial conflict. That's what happened in the spring of 1894 when the Baltimore Orioles arrived in Boston to play a routine baseball game. The game became anything but routine when a clash occurred between two players.

Within minutes both benches emptied to join the brawl. People in the grandstands decided to get involved, and the conflict between fans erupted. Someone set fire to the stands, and eventually the entire ballpark burned to the ground. To make matters worse, the fire spread to one hundred seven other Boston buildings. This unnecessary conflict turned into a community disaster.[2]

Conflicts are inevitable, but such devastating affects can be avoided. We bring different backgrounds, experiences, opinions, and emotions into our relationships. Whenever two people interact on an ongoing basis there is bound to be some discord. Having conflict need not be perceived as abnormal. The real issue is whether or not we get it resolved.

Past experiences certainly impact our present approaches to conflict. When I was growing up my two brothers and I would periodically get into arguments. My mother would immediately intercede, separate us, and tell us each to go to our rooms until we could learn to get along. Think about that a minute. "Go to your rooms until you can learn to get along." It is impossible to learn how to get along with people when you are separated from them. At any rate, when I encounter conflict today, my first reaction is to go to my room. Unfortunately, when I come out of my room the conflict is still waiting for me.

There's no magic solution for resolving conflict. There are, however a number of actions we can take to diffuse tense situations and move toward resolving the issues.

1. Strive for mutual benefit. The ridiculousness of selfish, unsettled disputes was exhibited years ago by a man in Cresco, Iowa. He made a half-car garage out of a one-car garage by hiring a contractor to saw the structure in half. The sawing was the climax to a property-line dispute between Halsted and the buyer of a small adjoining lot that Halsted sold. After the sale, it was learned that Halsted's garage straddled the line between the two properties. Negotiations over his use of the garage broke down, so he cut down the half that was not on his property.

There is no use pursuing resolution to any conflict unless you are willing to seek an agreement that is mutually beneficial. It's imperative for people to focus on what's right for people who are not right. I learned a long time ago that supposed winners in a conflict don't learn anything, and losers never forget who stepped on them to get their way. Make mutual benefit a priority.

2. Seek understanding. I am working on an invention that will revolutionize the world of negotiations. Once perfected, I predict this invention will eliminate conflict. What is it? An "Ego Enema." Countless relationship struggles would be solved if we could eliminate egos from the formula.

"If you don't agree with me," Sam Markewich said, "it means you haven't been listening."[3] His comment would indicate that there are basically two sides to any argument—our side, and the side that no intelligent, informed, breathing, sane, or self-respecting person could possibly hold. See what I mean about needing an Ego Enema?

Most people think they see the world as it is, but they don't. They see the world as they are. We perceive situations based on who we are, not the other person's perspective. Get inside of the other person. See the world the way he sees it. Be sensitive to other people's emotions. Feelings are neither right nor wrong—they are just feelings. But they are important to those who feel them! Accept people and their opinions where they are. Attempt to understand their perspective concerning the issues. Realize their priorities may not be yours, and the reasons behind their convictions could shed valuable light on the entire situation. Maintain calmness and patience as you listen to others talk. Allow for personal differences and move on.

3. Focus on the problem. Get the facts. Don't rely on assumptions. Anytime a conflict occurs, it is wise to make sure both parties are reading off the same page. Refrain from attacking people, and stay clear of arguing. Avoid fighting, battling, or trying to overcome another person's opinions or behavior. Insults, accusations, and blaming are dead-end strategies.

Aristotle had a good point. "How many a dispute could have been deflated into a single paragraph," he said, "if the disputants had dared to define their terms."[4] Resolution isn't possible by dealing with symptoms. Define your terms by first defining the problem. Please make sure you agree on what the *real* problem is.

4. Find a point of agreement. You've heard it said that sometimes people just need to learn to agree to disagree. That might be true, but I much prefer a different approach before resigning myself to that conclusion. Cullen Hightower said: "There's too much said for the sake of argument and too little said for the sake of agreement."[5] I like being around agreeable people with whom I can freely and openly discuss issues, concerns or topics that we don't necessarily agree on. Being agreeable involves the ability to smile, nod, and express respect for another person's position.

If you are intent on being disagreeable, other people will feel challenged and that their intelligence is being questioned. Telling someone he is flat-out wrong will immediately raise his defenses, heighten his stubbornness, and cause him to be more adamant about his position. How about agreeing to find out what we can agree on and committing our efforts to build on the things we can agree on and move beyond the disagreements?

There is an old saying that states, "Agree with thine adversary quickly."[6] Help others be right about as many things as possible, and you'll be amazed at how quickly the resistance will subside on other things.

5. Generate solutions. Don't get stuck dwelling on the problem. Just agree on it and then move on to the creatively stimulating process of generating solutions. "You cannot shake hands," said Indira Gandhi, "with a clenched fist."[7] Neither can you generate solutions to a disagreement with a one-track mind or a private agenda. What are *all* of the possible solutions that will produce a mutual benefit?

6. Determine a win-win plan of action. The motivation behind every conflict discussion should be to reach a point where we can genuinely agree on a solution that benefits each other. Give way on the minor points of disagreement that have become a thorn in the flesh. Look for major points of agreement that will be mutually beneficial. Find ways to nurture the other person's self-esteem. Be likable, respectful, and considerate rather than intimidating and demanding—you'll get much further. Try to love that person on the other end as you accept differences and capitalize on agreements.

Too often people approach arguments like the man who said to his coworker: "Okay, I'll meet you halfway. I will admit I'm right if you'll admit you're wrong."

An issue of "Pulpit Helps" included a humorous tale about a hunter who had his gun aimed at a large bear and was ready to pull the trigger. Just then the bear spoke in a soft, soothing voice, asking, "Isn't it better to talk than to shoot? Why don't we negotiate the matter? What is it you want?" The hunter lowered his rifle and answered, "I would like a fur coat." "That's good," said the bear. "I think that's something we can talk about. All I want is a full stomach; maybe we can reach a compromise." So they sat down to talk it over. A little while later the bear walked away alone. The negotiations had been successful—the bear had a full stomach, and the hunter had a fur coat![8]

This far-fetched fable embodies healthy advice for arriving at win-win solutions (although had I been the hunter I believe I would have spent a bit more time in the generating solutions stage). A great way to keep our horns unlocked is to start and end any discussion with these questions: "What is it the other person wants? How can both of our needs be met?"

> There comes a time in the affairs of man when you must take
> the bull by the tail and face the situation.
>
> —W. C. Fields[9]

Chapter 32

WORK THROUGH IT

Marriage is a mutual admiration society in which one person is always right, and the other is always the husband.

—W. Grant[1]

A HUSBAND AND WIFE WHO WERE having problems in their marriage asked their pastor for counsel. After a rather lengthy session with them, he realized that he wasn't making any progress in resolving their conflicts. Noticing a cat and a dog lying side by side in front of the fireplace, he said, "Look at how peaceful they are. They certainly don't see eye-to-eye on everything." The husband commented, "Yes, but just tie them together and see what happens!"

"A marriage without conflicts," said Andre Maurios, "is almost as inconceivable as a nation without crises."[2]

Maurios's comment reminded me of a judge who asked the husband in a divorce case, "Can you tell the court what passed between you and your wife during your heated argument that prompted the two of you to seek this separation?"

"I sure can, your honor," the man nervously responded, "there was a toaster, two knives, and a set of crystal."

Although amusing, this incident reminds us that conflict is normal and that marital wars can be dangerous.

Face it: the unique union of a man and woman is bound to create some issues of incompatibility. The transition from a casual to a formal relationship makes George Levinger's advice especially important. He said, "What counts in making a happy marriage is not so much how compatible you are, but how you deal with incompatibility."[3] Differences that existed before marriage are intensified when we live with them. We come from different backgrounds and personalities, see the world from unique perspectives, and are the unfortunate owners of irritating habits. We don't think alike, respond to life alike, or act alike. It can be frustrating. Rather than allowing the relationship to get tied up in knots, learn to loosen the noose a bit.

Author Charles Swindoll, writing in *Strike the Original Match*, discusses the reality of conflict in marriage. "There is no such thing as a home completely without conflicts. The last couple to live 'happily ever after' was Snow White and Prince Charming. Even though you are committed to your mate, there will still be times of tension, tears, struggle, disagreement, and impatience. Commitment doesn't erase our humanity! That's bad news, but it's realistic."[4]

Although normal, work through conflict. Don't allow your behaviors to elevate it.

Ogden Nash suggested: "To keep your marriage brimming with love in the loving cup, when you're wrong, admit it. When you're right, shut up."[5]

> There will always be a battle between the sexes because men and women want different things. Men want women, and women want men.
>
> —George Burns[6]

Section Nine

GRATITUDE

Chapter 33

KEEP THOSE FIRES BURNING

Husbands, take your wife on at least one date a week. It doesn't
have to be expensive (or fancy) but one that calls for dressing up
a little for each other and providing undisturbed time together.
—Ralph L. Byron[1]

IT'S NO SECRET THAT ROMANTIC gratification—or the lack
of it—are factors in every marriage. The idea of having one
date together a week is a great way to keep the romantic fires
burning. Undisturbed, private time allows you to be continually
reacquainted and in tune with each other's needs.

The following story provides a humorous look at one person's
experience:

> Mr. Smith came home from work early and found his wife in
> bed with a handsome young man. Just as Mr. Smith was about
> to storm out, she stopped him and said, "Before you leave, I'd
> like you to know how this happened.
>
> "When I was driving home from shopping this afternoon,
> I hit a hole in the pavement. The hole was filled with water.
> Great blobs of mud spattered all over this man. Without a trace

of anger, he looked at me and said, 'What rotten luck. I have a very important meeting this afternoon and just look at me!'

"I told him that I was terribly sorry and offered to clean him up. He seemed grateful, and I brought him home.

"He undressed in the bathroom, and I handed him the bathrobe I bought you for Christmas a few years ago. It no longer closes in front because of your potbelly.

"While his clothes were drying, I gave him lunch—the casserole you missed last night because you decided to go out with the guys after work. He said it was the best home-cooked meal he had had in months. I told him it was the first compliment I had received about my cooking in years.

"We talked while I pressed his shirt, and it was wonderful to have a conversation with a man who seemed interested in what I had to say. Suddenly he noticed the ironing board was wobbly. I had asked you a dozen times to fix it, but you were always too busy. The man fixed the ironing board in ten minutes, and then he actually put the tools away.

"As he was about to leave, he asked with a smile, 'Is there anything else your husband has neglected lately?' And that is the end of my story!"

James C. Dobson equals this story with one of his own. Dobson claimed he knew an obstetrician who was deaf and blind. It seemed the obstetrician had called a physician friend of Dobson's, asking for a favor.

"My wife has been having some abdominal problems, and she's in particular discomfort this afternoon," he said. "I don't want to treat my own wife and wonder if you'd see her for me."

The physician invited the doctor to bring his wife for an examination, whereupon he discovered [are you ready for this?] that she was five months pregnant! Her obstetrician husband was so busy caring for other patients that he hadn't even noticed his wife's burgeoning pregnancy. "I must admit wondering," said Dobson, "how in the world this woman ever got his attention long enough to conceive!"[2]

James Smith wrote, "The tragedy of western marriages is that most of us quit courting once we're married."[3]

What are you waiting for? Set the time now for your next date!

> The difference between courtship and marriage is the difference between the pictures in the seed catalog and what comes up.
>
> —James Wharton[4]

Chapter 34

HOW TO PHRASE IT WHEN
YOU WANT TO PRAISE IT

In spite of our supersonic generation, high-tech wizardry, and
computer gadgetry, there is no technical tool equal to praise.
—Jerry D. Twentier[1]

UPON ACCEPTING AN AWARD, JACK Benny once remarked,
"I really don't deserve this. But I have arthritis, and I don't
deserve that either."[2]

Wouldn't it be great if appreciation would become as natural to
give as undesirable life experiences were to contract? How many
times do small, seemingly insignificant actions go unnoticed? The
doers of such tasks feel they would be better off getting attention in
unacceptable ways.

Consider the employee who came in late one morning only to be
greeted by his supervisor who says, "Sam, you're late!"

Sam goes about his duties thinking, "So that's what I need to do to
get noticed. Day in and day out I do my job without anyone paying
any attention. Come in late and finally, they know I'm working here."

People want to believe their efforts deserve praise, and they are willing to go to great lengths to receive it. Yet, expressing appreciation is one of the most neglected acts in relationships. When you observe people doing good things, let them know you recognize it. How? Glad you asked. Here are some simple phrases that will help you praise people and encourage them to repeat their positive behavior:

"I appreciate the way you..."
"I'm impressed with..."
"You're terrific, because..."
"Thanks for going all out when you..."
"One of the things I enjoy most about you is..."
"I admire your..."
"Great job with..."
"I really enjoy working with you because..."
"Our team couldn't be successful without your..."
"Thank you for your..."
"You made my day when..."
"You can be proud of your..."
"You did an outstanding job of..."
"It's evident you have the ability to..."
"I like your..."
"You deserve a pat on the back for..."
"You should be proud of yourself for..."
"I admire the way you take the time to..."
"You're really good at..."
"You've got my support with..."
"What a great idea!"
"It's evident you have a special knack of..."
"You were a great help when..."
"You have a special gift for..."
"I enjoy being with you because you..."
"You're doing a top-notch job of..."

"It's fun watching you . . ."
"I know you can do it!"
"I believe in you."
"Your commitment to ＿＿＿＿＿ is appreciated!"

The power of positive praise is limited only by its lack of use. How many people do you know who could benefit from a sincere "congratulations" or "great job" or possibly even "you're the best"? Silent appreciation doesn't mean much. Let others know your positive regards toward them. They'll live up to your compliment.

Samuel Goldwyn said, "When someone does something good, applaud! You will make two people happy."[3] Take time to look through that list of phrases you can use to applaud people. Use them frequently. Find additional ways to praise and increase people's good feelings about themselves. You'll be happy you did.

> I believe that you should praise people whenever you can; it causes them to respond as a thirsty plant responds to water.
> —Mary Kay Ash[4]

Chapter 35

HAPPINESS IS LIVING
EVERY MOMENT

To experience happiness we must train ourselves to live in this moment, to savor it for what it is, not running ahead in anticipation of some future date nor lagging behind in the paralysis of the past.

—Luci Swindoll[1]

DENNIS WHOLEY, AUTHOR OF *Are You Happy?*, reported that according to expert opinion, perhaps only 20 percent of Americans are happy.[2] In another national survey, it was estimated that 29 percent of us are happy.

Regardless of the accuracy of these statistics, there is a pretty good indication that people want more in their lives. There is a hole somewhere waiting to be filled and thereby producing happiness. Actually, unhappy people simply have a gap between what they expect and what they are experiencing. That's why happiness has very little to do with what we attain. The more we get, the higher our expectations, and the more likely a larger gap will be created.

Unhappy people would probably agree with the wry definition of happiness offered by psychiatrist Thomas Szasz, who said,

"Happiness is an imaginary condition, formerly attributed by the living to the dead, now usually attributed by adults to children, and by children to adults."[3] According to this definition, happiness is anywhere we don't happen to be.

Former child star Shirley Temple Black told a story about her husband, Charles, and his mother. When Charles was a boy, he asked his mother what the happiest moment of her life was.

"This moment—right now," she responded.

"But what about all the other happy moments in your life?," he said, surprised. "What about when you were married?"

"My happiest moment then was then," she answered. "My happiest moment now is now. You can only really live in the moment you're in. So to me, that's always the happiest moment."[4]

I love Mrs. Black's perspective. Whenever you focus on the past, you strip the present of its beauty. And, when you get caught up in the future, you rob the present of its potential.

Happiness seems so simple—and yet, so difficult to define. Norman Cousins, former editor of *Saturday Review*, wrote, "Happiness is probably the easiest emotion to feel, the most elusive to create deliberately, and the most difficult to define. It is experienced differently by different people."[5] I suggest, after considerable thought, that happiness is an existing state of joyful contentment, accompanied by a peace about the present and hope for the future. Happiness is a by-product experienced by looking at all the good and bad in any given moment and then choosing to focus on the good—such an easy concept but a difficult habit to acquire.

"A happy person," said Hugh Downs of ABC's *20/20*, "is not a person in a certain set of circumstances, but rather a person with a certain set of attitudes."[6] Dr. Norman Vincent Peale agrees. "Happiness," he said, "is not a matter of good fortune or worldly possessions. It's a mental attitude. It comes from appreciating what we have, instead of being miserable about what we don't have. It's so simple—yet so hard for the human mind to comprehend."[7]

Here's a little help in developing the attitudes that nurture the seeds of happiness.

1. Accept life's difficulties. I know you know this, but let me remind you that life will never be void of problems. Pain and difficulty are constantly perched at your back door. They are inevitable experiences of living in an imperfect world. A great starting point to happiness is to accept these unpleasant experiences as quickly as you do the joys. To be content in the ups and downs of life epitomizes a truly happy person.

2. Choose happiness now. Waiting for your life to be totally in order before experiencing happiness is an unrealistic dream. "If only..." and "Someday I'll..." are detours to happiness. They snuff out contentment. The best part of your life is right now, not some day in the past or future. Life may not be as good as you want, but you really have it pretty good. Learn to be happy with what you have while you pursue all that you want.

3. Learn to look for the good. Try looking for the positives in your job, relationships, community, church, and children. Guard against focusing on the negatives or things that fall short of your expectations. Identify the little things that bring you a sprinkle of happiness. You'll be pleasantly surprised how developing a mindset that looks for the good prepares you to deal more positively with the problems you encounter.

4. Help others experience happiness. Bertrand Russell once said, "If there were in the world today any large number of people who desired their own happiness more than they desired the unhappiness of others, we could have a paradise in a few years."[8] Let go of judging. Accept people where they are. Expect the best from others. Help people believe in themselves. Become an inverse paranoid. You read that right. Inverse paranoids are people who think everyone is out to make them happy. Just imagine everyone you meet wanting to bring happiness to your life. And then try to do the same for them.

5. Decide what you want in life. In the early 1980s, two Harvard psychologists completed a study of people who called themselves happy.[9] And what did happy people have in common? Money? Success? Power? Health? Love?

None of the above.

Happy people had only two things in common: They knew exactly what they wanted, and they felt they were moving toward getting it. Dr. Benjamin Spock concurred. He said, "Happiness is mostly a by-product of doing what makes us feel fulfilled."[10] The ultimate in personal happiness is to be actively involved in something bigger than ourselves that causes us to stretch beyond where we are.

On the flip side, unhappiness can be experienced by not knowing what we want and working like crazy to get it. "Many persons have the wrong idea of what constitutes true happiness," advised Helen Keller. "It is not attained through self-gratification but through fidelity to a worthy purpose."[11]

Sometimes I think we work far too hard at trying to be happy. The more we pursue happiness, the more evasive it becomes. As Harold Kushner wrote in the best-selling book *When All You've Ever Wanted Isn't Enough*, "Happiness is a butterfly—the more you chase it, the more it flies away from you and hides. But stop chasing it, put away your net and busy yourself with other, more productive things than the pursuit of happiness, and it will sneak up on you from behind and perch on your shoulder."[12]

If you really want to be happy, the only person that can stop you is you. Don't strive to be happy. Be happy. Wake up each morning. Smile. Look for the good in the day. Choose to act happy. Find the good in others. Work toward something larger than yourself. Do the best you can in every endeavor.

Be encouraged by Denis Waitley's insight on happiness. "Happiness cannot be traveled to, owned, earned, worn, or consumed. Happiness is the spiritual experience of living every minute with love, grace, and gratitude."[13]

Just remember, happiness is having a poor memory about what happened yesterday.

—Lou Holtz[14]

Chapter 36

AN ETERNAL OPTIMIST

I've never seen a monument erected to a pessimist.

—Paul Harvey[1]

LUCILLE BALL ONCE SAID, "ONE of the things I learned the hard way was that it doesn't pay to get discouraged. Keeping busy and making optimism a way of life can restore your faith in yourself."[2]

Former President Ronald Reagan would certainly have agreed with Lucille Ball. He was an eternal optimist who was determined to make it a way of life. Richard Wirthlin, Reagan's pollster for seven years, relates a marvelous story that typifies Reagan's optimism.

Wirthlin said that in 1982, during an economic recession, Reagan's approval rating dropped to 32 percent, at that time the lowest on record for any president in the second year of office. Just a few months earlier his approval rating was incredibly in the low nineties—this was shortly after the attempted assassination.

Wirthlin visited the president in the Oval Office to update him on his status. "Tell me the news," Reagan said. Wirthlin hesitantly responded, "Not good." And Reagan replied, "What do you mean?"

Wirthlin then informed the president his approval rating was at 32 percent. Reagan was well aware of how bad that was for a second-year presidency, but he just smiled and said, "Dick, stop worrying, I'll just try to go out there and get shot again."[3]

The public display of our optimism is a natural expression of an internal condition. The more optimistic we are, the greater our chances of enduring the setbacks, challenges, and disappointments inherent in life. "If you are distressed by anything external," said Marcus Aurelius, "the pain is not due to the thing itself, but to your estimate of it; and this you have the power to revoke at any moment."[4] Do it!

> People with a negative attitude brighten the whole room when they leave.
>
> —Author unknown[5]

> An optimist thinks the glass is half full; a pessimist thinks the glass is half empty. A realist knows that if he sticks around, he's eventually going to have to wash the glass.
>
> —*Los Angeles Times* Syndicate[6]

Section Ten

GENEROSITY

Chapter 37

A TOUCH OF KINDNESS

People can do this for one another, can love one another with
understanding.

—Harold S. Kushner[1]

J ERRY JENKINS, WRITING FOR *Moody Monthly*, recalled a situation he observed while attending the premiere showing
of Francis Schaeffer's film, *How Should We Then Live?* Dr.
Schaeffer was fielding questions from the audience when a man
with cerebral palsy struggled to ask a question. His slow, broken
speech irritated people in the audience as they struggled to understand his words. But not Schaeffer.

"I'm sorry," Schaeffer responded as the man finished his question. "Would you please repeat your last three words?" The man
complied. "Now the last word one more time." The man again painstakingly repeated himself. Schaeffer went on to graciously answer
the man's question.

Then, to the dismay of the audience, the young man had a second
question. The entire process began again. Dr. Schaeffer continued

to work kindly and patiently answering the question to the man's satisfaction.[2]

What would have been your reaction? Dr. Schaeffer revealed a kindness that set an example for the entire audience. He treated the man who had a disability with the same dignity and respect given to others.

People don't care how much you know until you show them how much you care by your small acts of kindness. As you go about your daily activities, be especially sensitive to those who need your touch of kindness.

> Keep in mind that the true meaning of an individual is how he treats a person who can do him absolutely no good.
>
> —Ann Landers[3]

Chapter 38

AN ACT OF COMPASSION

How far you go in life depends on your being tender with the young, compassionate with the aged, sympathetic with the striving, and tolerant of the weak and strong—because someday in your life you will have been all of these.

—George Washington Carver[1]

As NEW YORK CITY'S MAYOR in 1935, Fiorello H. LaGuardia showed up in court one night in the poorest area of New York City. He suggested the judge go home for the evening as he took over the bench.

La Guardia's first case involved an elderly woman arrested for stealing bread. When asked whether she was innocent or guilty, this soft reply was offered, "I needed the bread, your honor, to feed my grandchildren." "I've no option but to punish you," the mayor responded. "Ten dollars or ten days in jail."

Proclaiming the sentence, he simultaneously threw ten dollars into his hat. He then fined every person in the courtroom fifty cents for living in a city "where a grandmother has to steal food to feed her grandchildren." Imagine the surprise of those in the room who,

I'm sure, thought this was a black-and-white, open-and-shut case. When all had contributed their fifty cents, the woman paid her fine and left the courtroom with an additional forty-seven dollars and fifty cents.[2]

It has been said that kindness is the oil that takes the friction out of life. So often it is easy to be grit, rather than oil, by judging, condemning, or berating those going through struggles. Yet, acts or words of kindness can cool the friction and help someone keep pressing on. Look around you. To whom will you show a kindness like that experienced by the grandmother?

> Kindness in words creates confidence; kindness in thinking creates profoundness; kindness in giving creates love.
>
> —Lao-tse[3]

Chapter 39

YOU CAN'T TAKE BACK THE WORDS

> There is so much good in the worst of us, and so much bad in the best of us, that it behooves all of us not to talk about the rest of us.
>
> —Robert Louis Stevenson[1]

I DON'T THINK THERE IS ANYTHING I despise worse than gossip. Gossips cause undue contention and strife. The wise King Solomon said, "The words of a whisperer are like dainty morsels, and they go down into the innermost parts of the body" (Prov. 26:22, NAS). Both the gossip and the unfortunate victim are injured by these "tiny morsels."

Listen to this conversation. Mary said, "Ellen told me you told her the secret that I asked you not to tell her." Alice responded, "Well, I told her I wouldn't tell you that she told me, so please don't tell her I did." Oh, what a tangled web we weave when we betray someone's trust.

There will always be people who believe everything they hear and feel compelled to repeat it. Gossips are simply people with a "sense of rumor." Don't be one of them.

I remember occasions when word got back to me concerning a betrayed confidence. What a devastating feeling. Trust was destroyed. Friendships are broken when the poisonous contents of a rumor leak.

Why do people gossip? Do we think we gain greater acceptance with peers? Does confidential information make us feel important, more knowledgeable, or superior so people will listen to us? Have you ever been jealous of somebody's achievements or the attention he receives and by pointing out his weaknesses you look a little better? If somebody has injured us, how easy it is to put him in a bad light as a way of retaliating and balancing the scales. Gossip can also be used to win others to our side during a conflict. There is a tendency to think that the more people we can get to agree with us, the healthier our self-worth is.

No matter what reason we give to excuse it, there is no reason to gossip!

There is a legend about a person who went to the village priest for advice after repeating some slander about a friend and then later found out it wasn't true. He asked the priest what he could do to make amends for his thoughtless act.

The priest told the man, "If you want to make peace with yourself, you must fill a bag with feathers and go to every door in the village, dropping a feather on each porch."

The peasant found a bag, filled it with feathers, and made his way throughout the village doing as he was told to do. He returned to the priest and asked, "What else can I do?"

"There is one more thing," responded the priest, "take your bag and gather up every feather."

The peasant reluctantly began his quest to gather all the feathers he had distributed. Hours later he returned, saying, "I could not find all the feathers, for the wind had blown them away."

The priest responded, "So it is with gossip. Unkind words are easily dropped but we can never take them back again."

The next time you are tempted to say an unkind, possibly untrue or unflattering word about someone, ask yourself how this information will benefit the receiver, yourself, and especially the person you are talking about. Be clear on this one irrefutable fact: once you say it, you can't take it back.

> A gossip is one who talks to you about others, a bore is one who talks to you about himself, and a brilliant conversationalist is one who talks to you about yourself.
>
> —Lisa Kirk[2]

Chapter 40

THE MYSTERY OF MONEY

A poor person who is unhappy is in a better position than a rich
person who is unhappy because the poor person has hope. He
thinks money will help.

—Jean Kerr[1]

ONEY IS A FASCINATING OBJECT. It is an emotionally
charged, highly personal, and often controversial topic.
There are people whose lives are driven by the accumulation of wealth. Other people receive immense satisfaction by seeing
how much they can give away. A select few are capable of achieving a
balance between the two. One thing is for sure: most of us show what
we believe and what we are by the way we handle what we have.

For many years, author George S. Clason entertained his readers
with short stories. In *Babylonian Parables,* he outlined the success
principles of famous ancient people and shared their philosophies
about finances. In their early stages, these stories were printed in
small booklets and distributed free to clients by banks, insurance
companies, and investment firms.

Eventually, Mr. Clason's stories became popular. He published a collection of his favorite selections in a book entitled, *The Richest Man in Babylon*. His book received impressive reviews and acclaim as an inspirational guide to financial planning.

Mr. Clason believed, "Babylon became the wealthiest city of the ancient world because its citizens were the richest people of their time. They appreciated the value of money. They practiced sound financial principles in acquiring money, keeping money, and making their money earn more money. They provided for themselves what we all desire... incomes for the future."[2] The Babylonians understood and respected the value of money without making it their driving value.

I wonder what people in the future will write about our generation's approach to and management of money. Recent financial conflict reminds us of our own drive toward money's values. Call me cynical, but I doubt we will be applauded for our financial wisdom. Look around you, and you'll spot a variety of practices and attitudes about money. Here are a few samples of what you might hear:

"I could be happy if I had more money." I've worked with people from a variety of walks of life. In seminar settings, I often hear people lament his or her choice of a low-paying career. I enjoy asking, "If your salary were doubled today, would you be fundamentally happier and more fulfilled?" The response of the majority is, "Of course!" My follow-up question tends to prompt further introspection. "How many of you are making substantially more money today than you were five years ago?" Many hands go up. "How many of you who answered yes are fundamentally happier, satisfied, and fulfilled?" The yes responses are practically non-existent.

The lesson: The more money you desire, the less satisfied you will be with what you have, because no matter how much you have, you can always want more. It's a vicious circle.

"I wish I could afford it." This phrase commonly flows from the mouths of people possessing a "poverty mentality." They want the world to think they're poor even though their salaries could afford them a comfortable lifestyle. Reckless spending, poor choices, and unreasonable expectations are frequently followed by complaints that they are living from paycheck to paycheck. Their financial attitudes and lifestyle have little rhyme or reason, yet they are convinced that "never having enough" is their destiny.

The lesson: You can't take people out of poverty until you take the poverty mentality out of people.

"Look at all the money I saved." Sale searchers live in a world of budgetary self-destruction. Rare is the person on the lookout for good deals who doesn't purchase more than they intended. The savings they could have had is lost by an emotional urge to save more money on unnecessary items. And, of course, their actions are justified by the good deal they found.

I'm reminded of the man who sat home anxiously waiting for his wife to return from the department store. He almost fainted when she walked in with both hands full of shopping bags. She threw a quick smile and remarked, "You told me not to get suckered into all the sales—so I bought everything at full price."

The lesson: The irony of a sale is that it is designed to get the consumer to make multiple purchases, resulting in more spending than if purchasing one item at full retail.

"Charge it!" According to Brian Harbour, author of *Living Obediently,* there are three categories of people in this world: "The haves, the have-nots, and the have-not-paid-for-what-they-haves."[3] Financial expert Larry Burkett estimates, "The average American family spends more than $2,000 a year on interest payments alone."[4] Our indulgence mentality could be represented by the man who told his wife, "We're going to start living within our income, even if we have to borrow the money to do it."

Rather than a convenience, credit cards have become a financial disaster waiting to happen. According to *Working Well,* "Nearly 75 percent of Americans who use credit cards make only the minimum payment each month. At that rate (minimum payments), you could spend the next thirty years paying back a $3,000 credit card debt and give the financial institution $8,000 worth of interest. It's the principle of compound interest in reverse."[5]

The lesson: It would be to your credit to think twice before you say "Charge it!"

"It's mine, all mine, and I plan to keep it." James Moffatt said, "A man's treatment of money is the most decisive test of his character—how he makes it and how he spends it."[6]

John M. Templeton is one of the most recognized financial experts in the world today. After his insightful lecture concerning his economic theories to the International Economics Convention, someone asked, "Mr. Templeton, do you have any tip for the best investment to make?"

He looked out, addressed the audience, and said, "I sure do. I can give you a risk-free guaranteed investment. It's one that I learned forty-six years ago, and it came from a book that's two thousand years old. It says, 'The first tenth of everything that you have you return to your storehouse.' You give it to God. And beyond that, you make offerings as God has prospered you." He said, "I'll guarantee you that will be the best investment you will ever make." Almost 50 percent of what Mr. Templeton has made goes into that investment.[7]

"It's not how much of my money will I give to God," said John Wesley, "but how much of God's money will I keep for myself?"[8]

The lesson: The true test of your attitude toward money is displayed in your willingness to share it.

The managing editor of *Money Magazine,* summing up a study his magazine conducted, concluded that money has become the number one obsession of Americans. "Money has become the new sex in this country."[9]

John Maxwell pointed out that some statistician found that the average person today has 484 wants or desires, compared to 72 a century ago. Of these, 94 can be classified as necessities, compared with 16 one hundred years ago. There were only 200 articles being offered for sale then, while today the total is well over 32,000.[10] This preoccupation with the mighty green and the quest for acquisition requires an individual check of our money perspective. How healthy is yours?

> Money is a wonderful servant but a terrible master. If it gets on top and you get under it, you will become its slave.
>
> —E. Stanley Jones[11]

Section Eleven

EMPATHY

Chapter 41

A Cure for Loneliness

We're all in this together, by ourselves.

—Lily Tomlin[1]

THE TRUTH IN LILY TOMLIN'S comment came to life in October of 1993 when the major television networks covered a story from Worcester, Massachusetts. Adele Gaboury died of natural causes at age seventy-three. Police found her body on her kitchen floor four years later.

Four years? How can any human being go unmissed for four years? According to the Associated Press, neighbors had notified authorities years earlier when they noticed an unusual amount of accumulated mail and newspapers and the lawn was virtually unkempt.

When the police notified Ms. Gaboury's brother, he indicated she had gone into a nursing home. Police notified the postal service to stop delivering mail. Neighbors stepped in to care for the yard. They had the utility company shut off the water when a frozen pipe broke and sent water flowing out under the door. No one suspected Ms. Gaboury's lifeless body was inside.

One friend from the past commented, "She didn't want anyone bothering her at all. I guess she got her wish, but it's awfully sad."

According to newspaper reports, Adele lived in her house in this middle-class neighborhood for forty years, but none of her neighbors knew her well. "My heart bleeds for her," a neighbor was quoted as saying, "but you can't blame a soul. If she saw you out there, she never said hello to you."[2]

I have to believe Adele Gaboury lived in a lonely world. She was surrounded by people, yet alone. Although it appears she made little effort to reach out to those around her, few people showered her with attention.

This unfortunate scenario reminds us that giving and receiving are interdependent. They work together to form the natural laws that govern our relationships. What we give to others, we'll get. What we send out comes back to us. What we sow, we reap. To borrow a saying, "What goes around comes around." Simply put, when you reach out to meet the needs of other people, your needs will be met.

We can learn a valuable lesson from Adele Gaboury's experience. What if Adele and her neighbors understood and lived out the natural laws? Smile. Be friendly. Offer assistance. Perform kind deeds. Be generous. Be nice. Show courtesy. Sharing love and a multitude of other gestures produces a like response. But, we must be willing to share these expressions to receive them.

A lonely life and unnoticed death are unnecessary. Be patient and persistent in seeking out opportunities to unselfishly give of yourself to meet the needs of others. Don't hesitate. "You cannot do a kindness too soon," said Ralph Waldo Emerson, "for you never know how soon it will be too late."[3]

Consider one final word of wisdom:

> Warmth, kindness, and friendship are the most yearned for commodities in the world. The person who can provide them will never be lonely.
>
> Ann Landers [4]

Chapter 42

MAKE A DIFFERENCE
IN PEOPLE'S LIVES

Doing nothing for others is the undoing of one's self. We must be purposely kind and generous or we miss the best part of existence. The heart that goes out of itself gets large and full of joy. This is the great secret of the inner life. We do ourselves the most good by doing something for others.

—Horace Mann[1]

A WISE AND BELOVED SHAH ONCE ruled the land of Persia. He cared deeply for his people and wanted only what was best for them. The Persians knew that this shah took a personal interest in their affairs, and they tried to understand how his decisions affected their lives. Periodically he would disguise himself and wander through the streets, trying to see life from their perspective.

One day he disguised himself as a poor village man and went to visit the public baths. Many people were there enjoying the fellowship and relaxation. The water for the baths was heated by a furnace in the cellar, where one man was responsible for maintaining the comfort level of the water. The shah made his way to the basement to visit with the man who tirelessly tended the fire.

The two men shared a meal together, and the shah befriended this lonely man. Day after day, week in and week out, the ruler went to visit the fire tender. The stranger soon became attached to his visitor because he came to where he was. No other person had showed that kind of caring or concern.

One day the shah revealed his true identity. It was a risky move, for he feared the man would ask him for special favors or for a gift. Instead, the leader's new friend looked into his eyes and said, "You left your comfortable palace and your glory to sit with me in this dungeon of darkness. You ate my bitter food and genuinely showed you cared about what happens to me. On other people you might bestow rich gifts, but to me you have given the best gift of all. You have given yourself."[2]

For thousands of years, people have been speculating on what constitutes quality human relationships. With all the philosophies, theories, and speculations, only one principle seems to stand strong. It is not new at all. In fact, it is almost as old as history itself. It was taught in Persia over three thousand years ago by Zoroaster to his fire worshipers. Confucius asserted the principle in China twenty-four centuries ago. In the Valley of Han lived the followers of Taoism. Their leader, Lao-Tzu, taught the principle incessantly. Five hundred years before Christ, Buddha taught it to his disciples on the banks of the holy Ganges River. The collections of Hinduism contained this principle over fifteen hundred years before Christ. Nineteen centuries ago, Jesus taught His disciples and followers much the same principle. He summed it up in one thought: "Do to others as you would have them do to you" (Luke 6:31, NIV).

Unselfishly giving of ourselves probably wouldn't make a primary course of study in the school of success. Although we make a living by what we get, the true rewards are experienced because of what we give. You have not really lived a fulfilled day, even though you may be a success by societal standards, unless you have done something for someone who will never be able to repay you.

In the midst of your flurry of activities in this competitive, go-get-'em world, reflect on Rabbi Harold Kushner's thoughts: "The purpose of life is not to win. It is to grow and to share. You will get more satisfaction from the pleasure you have brought into other people's lives than you will from the times you outdid and defeated them."[3]

> If you wish others to respect you, you must show respect for them...Everyone wants to feel that he counts for something and is important to someone. Invariably, people will give their love, respect and attention to the person who fills that need. Consideration for others generally reflects faith in self and faith in others.
>
> —Ari Kiev[4]

Chapter 43

GETTING EVEN

You will find as you look back upon your life that the moments
that stand out, the moments when you have really lived, are the
moments when you have done things in a spirit of love.

—Henry Drummond[1]

D
URING THE DAYS OF THE Berlin Wall, a few East Berliners
decided to send their West Berlin neighbors a "gift."
They proceeded to load a dump truck with undesirables,
including garbage, broken bricks, building material, and any other
disgusting items they could find. They calmly drove across the
border, received clearance, and delivered their present by dumping
it on the West Berlin side.

Needless to say, the West Berliners were irritated and intent on
"getting even." People immediately began offering ideas on how
to out-do the repulsive actions of their adversaries. A wise man
interrupted their angry reactions and offered an entirely different
approach. Surprisingly, people responded favorably to his suggestions and began loading a dump truck full of essential items that
were scarce in East Berlin. Clothes, food, and medical supplies

poured in. They drove the loaded truck across the border, carefully unloaded and stacked the precious commodities, then left a sign that read, "Each gives according to his ability to give."[2]

Imagine the reaction of those who saw the "payback" and powerful message on the sign. Shock. Embarrassment. Distrust. Unbelief. Maybe even a bit of regret.

What we give to others sends a loud message about who we are. How we respond to unkindness, unfairness, or ingratitude reveals our true character.

> Shall we make a new rule of life from tonight: always to try to be a little kinder than is necessary.
>
> —James M. Barrie[3]

Chapter 44

NEVER ASSUME YOU'RE
PEDALING TOGETHER

We are born for cooperation, as are the feet, the hands, the
eyelids and the upper and lower jaws. People need each other
to make up for what each one does not have.

—Marcus Aurelius[1]

T HE DEFINITION OF THE WORD *cooperation* stems from two
Latin words, *co*, meaning "with," and *opus*, meaning "work."
So, quite literally, cooperation means working with others.
Sounds simple, doesn't it?

For over twenty-five years the *Des Moines Register* newspaper
has sponsored a summer Register's Annual Great Bike Ride Across
Iowa (RAGBRAI). Bikers from all over the country emerge on the
western side of Iowa, determined to be one of hundreds of successful
riders who invest a week pedaling their way across the state.

One year, RAGBRAI designated our community as a stopping
point for the night. It was an incredible site to watch the bikers
swarm into town and set up camp. Young and old alike enjoyed the
challenge, fellowship, and fun that accompanied this popular event.

As I walked through one of the camping areas, I overheard a conversation between two riders who were navigating the trail together on a tandem bike. The man was complaining about the difficulty of one of the hills they had to climb earlier in the day. "That was a struggle," he said. "I thought for sure we were going to have to push the bike up the hill on foot."

"It sure was a steep hill," his female companion responded, "and if I hadn't kept the brake on all the way, we would have rolled back down for sure."

There's practically no limit to what people can accomplish when they work cooperatively. However, if just one person drags his feet or continually applies the brake, everyone else suffers. Married couples, departments at work, athletic teams, bands, boards, dancers, or the cast in a play need to understand where the team is going, how they will get there, and what effort will be required by each person.

When riding a bike together, remember to peddle together. Work with a spirit of cooperation.

> The purpose of life is to collaborate for a common cause; the problem is nobody seems to know what it is.
> —Gerhard Gschwandtner[2]

Section Twelve

HOPE

Chapter 45

YOU CAN MAKE A DIFFERENCE

Even the Lone Ranger didn't do it alone

—Harvey Mackay[1]

ONGRATULATIONS! YOUR DECISION TO PURCHASE and read this book represents an admirable commitment to positively impact peoples' lives. Keep going. Only a few stories left. The final pages could transform your life as well as the lives of those around you. So, read on.Let's suppose for a moment you just received a card in the mail from your best friend. The message went like this:

> *First, I want to apologize. I've intended to send you this card for several months but never got around to it.*
>
> *You are a special person! I appreciate your acceptance of me just the way I am, and your friendship is the most valuable thing I have. I marvel at your positive attitude toward work, family, and life in general. It shows in everything you do. Thank you for being an exemplary role model. Most of all, I appreciate you for being you.*
>
> *Have a great day!*

How would you feel? Would you sense a tinge of embarrassment along with a broad internal smile? How might this note affect your day, your interactions at work, or your feelings about yourself? Most important, how many times have you sent or received such an encouraging message?

Contrast that uplifting scenario with the reality of how many people feel about their relationships.

Clare Booth Luce wrote a poignant article for *Life* magazine entitled, "What Really Killed Marilyn: The 'Love Goddess' Who Never Found Any Love." Luce suggests that the dangling phone [found next to her body] was an apt symbol of Marilyn's life. She tried for a long time to say that she was a person, but few ever took her seriously. Only after her death on a Saturday night, when all beautiful women are assumed to be out on the arm of a handsome escort, did many of the facts of her life surface.

> Marilyn Monroe was seriously disliked by most of her Hollywood contemporaries. She was dubbed a 'prima donna.' Very often, she would arrive hours late for a filming. As she casually strolled into the studio, no one suspected that she had been at her home nervously vomiting. She was terrified, afraid of cameras. No doubt her emotional reactions were the result of a sad and troubled childhood. Her father, an itinerant baker, had deserted the family. Her mother was repeatedly committed to mental institutions. Marilyn was raped at age eight by a boarder in her foster home. She was given a nickel not to tell.
>
> Now at age 35, her mirror kept telling her that the only thing others ever noticed about or praised in her was fading. She must have felt like an artist who was losing his vision or a musician whose hands were becoming arthritic. Marilyn had endured a painful childhood, had moved through several marriages, and had made many movies, but few ever took her seriously... until she was dead."[3]

We need each other! Yet we live in an age where actions of kindness and encouragement are far too rare. We have a tendency to nitpick and find fault. Positive, uplifting messages are buried in the desire to make people what we want them to be rather than appreciating them for who they are.

Throughout this book we have offered a road map leading to a lifestyle of enriching others. No shortcuts. No detours. No back roads to speed up your trip. Once you commit yourself to the journey, you'll experience methods for making the trip a pleasurable one.

These techniques and ideas have surfaced from my experiences and the experiences of many people who have shown me how to successfully practice a lifestyle of building up people. So pursue the principles you've read. You'll be entertained, inspired, and challenged to refine your people-buliding skills so you can make a positive difference in people's lives.

> Lonliness and the feeling of being unwanted is the most terrible poverty.
>
> —Mother Teresa[4]

Chapter 46

HOW DO PEOPLE FEEL AROUND YOU?

People love others not for who they are but for how they make us feel.

—Irwin Federman[1]

I WISH YOU COULD MEET MY daughter. Katy is a vibrant, enthusiastic, young lady with a fabulous approach toward life. As a fourth grader, she committed herself to an enviable work ethic, developed a magnetic personality, and endeared the respect of her teacher. (Of course, I'm entirely objective about my assessment.)

At the end of Katy's first semester as a fourth grader, a parent-teacher conference was scheduled for Thursday afternoon at 4:30 p.m. She was especially excitable during the week and confirmed the meeting time with her mother and me on several occasions. We assured her that both of us planned to attend this special event.

On Wednesday morning, Katy approached her teacher before school started. "I sure wish my conference was today!" she exclaimed.

"Isn't tomorrow a good day for your parents to come?" her insightful teacher, Mrs. DeJong, queried.

"Oh no, they'll both be here," Katy responded, "I just wish my conference was today."

Fascinated by this unusual student attitude, Mrs. DeJong probed further. "Why would you like me to meet with your parents today, Katy?"

Katy flashed one of her heartwarming smiles as she blurted, "I just can't wait for them to come home and tell me how good I am!"

Being a good student, Katy knew the parent-teacher conference was one avenue for her to receive a bit of recognition. She also knew that my wife and I made it a habit to discuss the conference with the kids. It didn't take a rocket scientist to see why Katy was anxious for her conference. This was her opportunity to hear how good she was, even though she already knew.

My wife and I have ample reason to support and encourage our children. They are good kids. I'm concerned that I spend far too little time looking for ways to encourage and an excessive amount of time searching for things to correct. It's amazing how conditioned I've become—conditioned to believe a parent's role is to correct, discipline, and direct. I'm fine with that when balanced with support, recognition, and encouragement. Oh, to find that perfect balance.

Encouragers do what? Build our hopes. Support our dreams. Understand our difficulties. Recognize our efforts. Celebrate with us in our achievements. Keep us from going to bed with an aching stomach, broken heart, or damaged spirit. They know what to say and when to say it. Encouragers provide nourishment for the soul.

Become an encourager. Make it possible for people to say, "I like myself better when I'm with you."

> Three billion people on the face of the earth go to bed hungry every night, but four billion people go to bed hungry for a simple word of encouragement and recognition.
>
> —Cavett Robert[2]

Chapter 47

GIVE YOURSELF AWAY

Only those who have learned the power of sincere and selfless contribution experience life's deepest joy: true fulfillment.

—Anthony Robbins[1]

THERE ARE TWO SEAS IN the Holy Land. The famous Sea of Galilee takes in fresh water from a nearby brook, uses it to generate a variety of marine vegetation, and then passes it on to the Jordan River. The Jordan does its part by spreading the life throughout the desert, turning it into fertile land.

The Dead Sea, on the other hand, comes by its name for a reason— it's dead. The water in the Dead Sea is so full of salt that no life can exist. The major difference between these two bodies of water is that the Dead Sea takes in the water from the Jordan River and hangs on to it. It has no outlet.

What a perfect example of the differences in people. People who live without giving themselves away become stagnant. What they keep stifles them. Those who freely give of themselves multiply life. Eric Butterworth said, "A committed giver is an incurably happy person, a secure person, a satisfied person, and a prosperous person."[2]

There's a life-enhancing lesson here. If you don't sow anything today, you'll have nothing to reap in the future. A rich life is the direct result of enriching others. "Don't judge each day by the harvest you reap," advised Robert Louis Stevenson, "but by the seeds that you plant."[3]

According to the *New York Times,* Mr. Milton Petrie enjoyed giving his money away. Petrie, the son of a Russian immigrant pawn shop owner, researched New York papers "for stories of people life had kicked in the face. He then reached for his checkbook."

Petrie built his fortune with a chain of women's clothing stores. His lifelong commitment to generous giving continued even after he died at age ninety-two. The newspaper headline reporting his death said: "Millionaire's Death Doesn't Stop His Generosity." His will reportedly named four hundred fifty-one beneficiaries of his $800 million estate.[4]

"What keeps our interest in life and makes us look forward to tomorrow is giving pleasure to other people," advised Eleanor Roosevelt. "Happiness is not a goal, it is a by-product."[5]

Did you know that Elvis Presley never took a tax deduction for his donations to charities, believing it violated the spirit of giving?[6]

General William Booth had a passion for the poor of London and committed himself to a mission of meeting those needs. By the time of his death, Booth's local mission had spread across the world. His final sermon, delivered from a hospital bed to an international convention of Salvation Army "soldiers," was simply a one-word telegram that read: "Others!"[7]

Booth's one-word sermon encapsulated everything he believed about the purpose of living—giving unselfishly of yourself to benefit others.

Billionaire John D. Rockefeller, Sr. lived the first part of his life as a miserable man, unable to sleep, feeling unloved, and surrounded by bodyguards. At age fifty-three, he was diagnosed with a rare disease. He lost all of his hair, and his body became shrunken. Medical experts gave him a year to live.

Rockefeller started thinking beyond his current life and sought meaning to his existence. He gave away his money to churches and the poor, and he established the Rockefeller Foundation. His life turned around, his health improved and, contrary to the doctor's prediction, he lived to be ninety-eight.[8]

John D. Rockefeller's life exemplified the transformation that's possible when the joy of giving is discovered. You might be tempted to think that if you had Rockefeller's wealth, giving to others would be easy. Although it's easy to find examples of people with wealth who gave it away, what we're talking about here is much more than writing a check to your favorite charity. That's only a tiny portion of the message.

"Every person passing through life will unknowingly leave something and take something away," reflected Robert Fulghum. "Most of this 'something' cannot be seen or heard or numbered or scientifically detected or counted . . . The census doesn't count it. Nothing counts without it."[9]

People like John Wesley make Fulghum's "something" a way of life. Wesley said, "Do all the good you can, in all the ways you can, to all the souls you can, in every place you can, at all the times you can, with all the zeal you can, as long as ever you can."[10]

You can keep the waters of life flowing and add tremendous value by giving yourself to others. Put others first in your thinking. Find ways to enrich their lives. Give unselfishly. It is a natural law of life that the more of yourself that you pass on to others with no expectation of receiving in return, the more your life will be blessed.

If you want to experience ongoing success, learn to give yourself away. "Success is not rare. It is common," believed Henry Ford, Sr. "It is not a matter of luck or of contesting, for certainly no success can come from preventing the success of another. It is a matter of adjusting one's efforts to overcome obstacles and one's abilities to give the services needed by others. There is no other possible success. Most people think of it in terms of getting; success, however, begins in terms of giving."[11]

Lock your house, go across the railroad tracks, find someone in need, and do something for him.

—Dr. Karl Menninger[12]

Chapter 48

ONE THING AT A TIME

The great dividing line between success and failure can be expressed in five words: "I did not have time."
—Franklin Field[1]

TIME IS AN UNCONTROLLABLE, IRREVERSIBLE, previous commodity. It is an equal opportunity element for every person. It is spent one second at a time—never to be saved or retrieved—only invested wisely. All those little decisions about how to invest your time accumulate into a larger investment called life.

Multiple priorities are the order of the day. Downsizing, cutbacks, expansion, reorganization, and other corporate movements are increasing the demands on people. Yet, few of us possess the ability to deal with multiple priorities at the same time.

Announcing our busyness and scrambling to attend to several projects at the same time is a surefire formula for frustration. Step back. Evaluate. Set your wheels in motion to take one thing at a time.

In the midst of life's most demanding moments, I often reflect on a childhood fascination: the plate spinner. I remember the juggler on the *Ed Sullivan Show* spinning those white plates on wobbly sticks.

He was an artist at building drama into his performance. First one, then two, then six plates would be spinning. The performer would momentarily lose track of the first plates now on the verge of doom.

The audience would yell, "Look out!" and the performer would quickly attend to the plates in danger of falling. Normally, a few plates would smash to the floor as the juggler feverishly ran from one to the other until all plates were successfully spinning in their rightful places and spinning smoothly.

Isn't that how you often feel about your life? Hurrying here and there, running faster and faster to keep those activities spinning, and everybody was happy responding to their "look outs"? Even when you've done your best to keep up, something important ultimately seems to tumble and break into pieces.

You keep running, hoping to pick up the pieces later. The rapid pace continues until retiring into bed, exhausted and unable to rest, thinking about the juggling you'll be required to perform when the sun comes up. And on and on and on. Juggling becomes a way of coping with the external demands of others and the internal needs for personal excellence, relationships, and time for self.

Plate spinning is an exciting juggling act, but juggling the demands of life can be managed with a more strategic approach. You have a choice to make. Remaining in a state of constant crisis intervention is anti-productive. It is a vicious cycle broken only by the one who is responsible for the plates.

Focused concentration and effort on a single task is the closest you can get to maximum effectiveness. Attempting to do several things at once blurs your focus and disables your concentration. Single-minded attention on one task is a hallmark of effective people. Do one thing at a time. Do it completely. Do it in a timely manner—*now*.

> Getting your house in order and reducing the confusion gives you more control over your life. Personal organization some how releases or frees you to operate more effectively.
>
> —Larry King[2]

NOTES

SECTION ONE: LOVE

Chapter 1: Good Advice—Wrong Application

1. Leo F. Buscaglia, *Loving Each Other* (New York: Random House, Inc.), 171.

2. Theodore Rubin, *One to One,* quoted in *Loving Each Other,* p. 188.

3. Fred Allen, http://www.brainyquote.com/quotes/quotes/f/ fredallen100374.html (accessed February 1, 2009).

Chapter 2: The Flip Side of Love

1. Katherine Hepburn, http://www.brainyquote.com/quotes/quotes/k/ katharineh140351.html.

2. Karl Menninger, Source unknown.

Chapter 3: Making Acts of Love No Matter How We Feel

1. Tom Mullen, Source unknown.

2. Dr. Joyce Brothers quoted from *The Power of Fate,* by Gisele G Barbosa, © 2007.

3. Anita Taylor and Dr. Robert Taylor, *Couples: The Art of Staying Together* (Washington: Acropolis Books, 1978).

4. *U.S. News & World Report.*

5. George W. Crane, *Psychology Applied.*

6. Robin Marantz Henig, *USA Today,* August 5, 1998.

Chapter 4: What Does Love Look Like?

1. Saint Augustine, http://www.brainyquote.com/quotes/quotes/s/saintaugus148553.html (accessed February 1, 2009)

2. Melanie Clark, http://www.quotations.me.uk/famous-love-quotations-quotes/23-love-quote.htm (accessed February 1, 2009).

3. *Fiddler on the Roof*, 1971, http://zemerl.com/cgi-bin//show.pl?title=Do+You+Love+Me%3F+(from+Fiddler+on+the+Roof) (accessed February 2, 2009).

4. Ida Fay Oglesby, *P.E.O. Record*, January, 1983, http://www.funnysermons.com.

5. John Roach and Mary Sweeney, *The Straight Story*, Hyperion Books, 1999.

6. http://www.preaching.com/resources/from_the_lectionary/11563713/page11/premium/archive11/ (accessed February 13, 2009).

7. Helen Keller, http://www.brainyquote.com/quotes/quotes/h/helenkelle143024.html (accessed February 3, 2009).

Section Two: Acceptance

Chapter 5: My Wife Is Always Right

1. Max Gunther, http://quotationsbook.com/author/3095/ (accessed February 3, 2009).

2. Jonathan Kozol, http://www.quotationspage.com/quote/2325.html (accessed February 3, 2009).

3. H. L. Mencken, http://www.quotes.net/authors/Henry+Louis+Mencken (accessed February 3, 2009).

4. Ben Franklin, //quote.robertgenn.com/auth_search.php?authid=286 (accessed February 3, 2009).

5. Sydney J. Harris, http://quotationsbook.com/quote/add_to_site/2902/ (accessed February 3, 2009).

Chapter 6: Huggable and Buggable

1. Maurice Wagner http://quotationsbook.com/quote/2827/ (accessed February 4, 2009)

2. Eugene Kennedy, http://abebblog.blogspot.com/2008_06_01_archive.html.

Chapter 7: Creating a Relationship Masterpiece

1. David Viscott, http://quotesblog.blogspot.com/2003_04_01_archive.html (accessed February 15, 2009)

2. Gary Shandling, http://www.geocities.com/tangental/quotes17.htm (accessed February 15, 2009).

Chapter 8: A Proposition for You

1. Franklin P. Jones, http://www.people.ubr.com/authors/by-first-name/f/franklin-p-jones/franklin-p-jones-quotes/whoever-thinks.aspx (accessed February 16, 2009).

2. Michelle Gelman, Source unknown.

3. Julius Gordon, Source unknown.

4. Lady Bird Johnson, http://koti.mbnet.fi/neptunia/politics/ladyb1.htm (accessed February 16, 2009).

5. Dr. Joyce Brothers, http://thinkexist.com/quotation/marriage_is_not_just_spiritual_communion_and/170004.html (accessed February 16, 2009).

6. Mark Beltaire, www.meaningfulmarriages.com/60.html (accessed February 16. 2009).

7. John Stevenson, http://www.weddingphotographermoncton.com/marriage_quotes.htm (acessed February 16, 2009).

8. George Bernard Shaw, http://www.brainyquote.com/words/ma/maximum188555.html (accessed February 16, 2009).

9. Sydney Smith, http://www.brainyquote.com/quotes/authors/s/sydney_smith.html (accessed February 16, 2009).

10. Joe Murray, http://www.worldofquotes.com/topic/Marriage/1/index.html (accessed February 16, 2009).

11. Dr. Joyce Brothers, *Forbes*, (CA: Forbes Inc., 1991), 160.

12. Kathy Mohnke, http://www.quotes.net/authors/Kathy+Mohnke (accessed February 16, 2009).

13. Katherine Hepburn, http://www.quoteworld.org/quotes/6481 (accessed February 16, 2009).

14. Benjamin Franklin, quotationsbook.com/quote/25387/ (accessed February 16, 2009).

15. Barbara Bush, commencement address at Severance Green, Wellesley College, Wellesley, Massachusetts, June 1, 1990.

16. Abigail Van Buren, http://www.quotationspage.com/quote/21629.html (accessed February 16, 2009).

17. Martin Luther, http://quotationsbook.com/quote/25451/ (accessed February 16, 2009).

18. Erma Bombeck, http://www.quotes.net/quote/11022 (accessed February 16, 2009).

19. George Burns, http://www.imdb.com/name/nm0122675/bio (accessed February 16, 2009).

20. Agatha Christie, http://www.brainyquote.com/quotes/authors/a/agatha_christie.html (accessed February 16, 2009)

21. Cher, http://www.brainyquote.com/quotes/authors/c/cher.html (accessed February 16, 2009).

22. Henny Youngman, http://www.latestngreatest.net/funny_marriage_quotes.htm (accessed February 16, 2009).

23. J. Grant Howard, Jr. quote, Source unknown.

24. Benjamin Disraeli, http://www.brainyquote.com/words/am/amiable129568.html (accessed February 16, 2009).

25. Mark Twain, http://quotationsbook.com/quote/14228/ (accessed February 16, 2009).

26. Rev. Theodore Hesburgh, http://www.allgreatquotes.com/mothers_day_quotes20.shtml (accessed February 16, 2009).

27. Doug Larson, http://www.brainyquote.com/quotes/authors/d/doug_larson.html (accessed February 16, 2009).

28. Ann Landers, Source unknown.

29. Rodney Dangerfield, https://www.brainyquote.com/quotes/quotes/r/rodneydang131987.html (accessed February 16, 2009).

30. Stanislaus Leszcynski quote, Source unknown.

Section Three: Forgiveness

Chapter 9: Keep Your Bridges in Good Repair

1. Thomas Fuller, http://www.whatquote.com/quotes/Thomas-Fuller/781-He-that-cannot-forgi.htm (accesssed February 17, 2009).

2. John Wesley, quoted in *The Friendship Factor*, Alan Loy McGinnis (Augsburg Books, 2004), 172.

3. Robin Casarjian, *Forgiveness: A Bold Choice for a Peaceful Heart* (New York: Bantam Books), 135.

4. Napoleon Hill, Source unknown.

5. Clara Barton, quoted in *The Life of Clara Barton*, William Eleazar Barton (Cambridge, MA: The Riverside Press, 1922), 345.

6. Elbert Hubbard, quoted in *Talent Is Never Enough Workbook,* John C. Maxwell (Nashville, TN: Thomas Nelson, Inc., 2007), 46.

7. Martin Luther King, Jr. quoted in *25 Ways to Win With People,* John C. Maxwell and Les Parrott, Ph.d. (Nashville, TN: Thomas Nelson, Inc., 2005), 83.

8. Samuel Goldwyn quoted in *The Power of Influence,* John C. Maxwell (David C. Cook, 2001).

Chapter 10: Placing People in Proper Perspective

1. Joshua Loth Liebman, quote, http://www.quoteland.com/topic. asp?CATEGORY_ID=3 (accessed February 18, 2007).

2. *Inventing a Voice,* by Molly Meijer Wertheimer (Lantham, MD: Rowman and Littlefield Publishers, Inc., 2004), 405.

3. Barbara Bush quote, *Laura Bush,* by Robert P. Watson (Hauppauge, NY: Nova Science Publishers, Inc., 2005), 158.

4. Antoine de Saint-Exupery, http://www.famousquotesandauthors. com/authors/antoine_de_saint_exupery_quotes.html (accessed February 16, 2008).

5. Harold Kushner, *When All You've Ever Wanted Isn't Enough* (New York, NY: Kushner Enterprises, Inc.), 165.

6. Barbara Walters, Source unknown.

Chapter 11: Be Willing to Say "I'm Sorry"

1. Erik H. Erikson, *Young Man Luther* (New York, NY: W.W. Norton & Co., 1962), 70.

2. *Sunshine* magazine, Source unknown.

Chapter 12: Let Go of the Past

1. William Arthur Ward, http://thinkexist.com/quotation/forgiveness_ is_the_key_that_unlocks_the_door_of/330854.html (accessed February 17, 2009).

2. Corrie ten Boom, *Tramp for the Lord* (Berkley, 1978), 53–55.

3. Mahatma Gandhi, http://quotationsbook.com/quote/15510/ (accessed Februrary17, 2009).

4. Ernest Hemingway, *The Complete Short Stories of Ernest Hemingway* (New York, NY: Simon & Schuster, 1998), 29.

5. Brian Tracy, *Maximum Achievement* (New York, NY: Simon & Schuster, 1993), 338.

6. Laurence Sterne, http://quotes.maxabout.com/authors/l/laurence_sterne.aspx (accessed February 18, 2009).

7. Patti Davis, *Angels Don't Die* (New York: HarperCollins Publishers, 1995).

8. Benjamin Franklin, http://www.ushistory.org/Franklin/quotable/singlehtml.htm (accessed February 18, 2009).

Section Four: Kindness

Chapter 13: Enlarge Your Circle of Influence

1. Dale Carnegie, *How to Win Friends and Influence People* (New York: Simon & Schuster, 1981), 52.

2. Marcus Aurelius, quoted by Dale Carnegie, *How to Stop Worrying and Start Living* (New York: Simon and Schuster, 2004), 121.

3. Albert Einstein, http://thinkexist.com/quotation/strange_is_our_situation_here_upon_earth-each_of/8534.html (accessed February 18, 2009).

Chapter 14: Beware of Becoming a Fault-Finder

1. Kahlil Gibran, http://www.quotesnsayings.com/kahlil-gibran/ (accessed February 18, 2009).

2. Charlie Brown, quoted by John C. Maxwell, *Be a People Person* (David C. Cook, 2007), 54.

3. Will Rogers, quoted by John C. Maxwell, *Be a People Person* (David C. Cook, 2007), 155.

4. Kahlil Gibran, *The Kahlil Gibran Reader* (New York, Citadel Press, 2006), 39.

5. Confucius, http://quotationsbook.com/quote/7596/ (accessed February 18, 2009).

6. John Wanamaker, quoted in Dale Carnegie, *How to Win Friends and Influence People*, (New York, Simon and Schuster, Inc., 1981), 5.

7. Lord Chesterfield, quoted by Aaron Ben-Ze'ev, *The Subtlety of Emotions* (Cambridge, MA: The MIT Press, 2001), 395.

8. Thomas Cogswell Upham, *Life, Religious Opinions and Experience of Madame Guyon* (New York, 1854).

9. Alice Duer Miller, http://www.wise-quotes.com/quotes-topic/friendship (accessed February 18, 2009).

10. Abraham Lincoln, quoted by Warren W. Wiersbe, *The Wiersbe Bible Commentary: Old Testament* (David C. Cook, 2007), 843.

11. Tyne Daly, http://www.finestquotes.com/select_quote-category-Criticism-page-0.htm (accessed February 18, 2009).

Chapter 15: Don't Overlook Little Acts of Kindness

1. Mother Teresa, quoted by Glenna Hammer Moulthrop, *Mother Teresa: Living in Love* (Nashville, TN: TowleHouse Pub. Co., 2000).

2. Claude M. Fuess, *Calvin Coolidge—The Man From Vermont* (Boston, Little, Brown and Companhy, 1940), 491.

3. Rita Snowden, Source unknown.

4. William Arthur Ward, http://thinkexist.com/quotation/a_warm_smile_is_the_universal_language_of/8445.html (accessed February 18, 2009).

5. St. Ambrose, http://quotationsbook.com/quote/2779/ (accessed February 18, 2009).

6. Mother Teresa, http://74.125.95.132/search?q=cache:TkWe3VbSWBOJ:www.stgregorys.cg.catholic.edu.au/newsletters/term_three/Term3Week7Newsletter2008.pdf+%22Spread+your+love+everywhere+you+go,+first+of+all+in+your+own+house%22%22&hl=en&ct=clnk&cd=1&gl=us (accessed February 19, 2009).

7. Mark Twain and Justin Kaplan, *Great Short Works of Mark Twain* (Harper Collins, 2004), 333.

Chapter 16: Kindness as a Lifestyle

1. Barbara Bush, http://thinkexist.com/quotation/never_lose_sight_of_the_fact_that_the_most/255457.html (accessed February 19, 2009).

2. Chuck Wall, *St. Petersburg Times,* St. Petersburg, FL, October 29, 1993.

3. *The Wausau Daily Herald,* Landers, Ann. "Random acts of kindness rampant." "Contra Costa Times" September 13, 1995, Sec. F:5.

4. John Wanamaker, http://quotationsbook.com/quote/25288/ (accessed February 19, 2009).

Section Five: Friendship

Chapter 17: Portrait of a Friendship

1. John R. O'Neil, www.goodnewsbroadcast.com/black/samaritans.html (accessed February 19, 2009).

2. *Book of Sunshine,* Source unknown.

3. Henry Ford, http://en.thinkexist.com/quotation/my_best_friend_ is_the_one_who_brings_out_the_best/13638.html (accessed February 19,2009).

4. Joan Baez, http://www.quotationspage.com/quotes/Joan_Baez/ (accessed February 19, 2009).

Chapter 18: Develop the Ability to Ask Questions

1. Chinese Proverb. http://thinkexist.com/quotation/he_who_asks_a_ question_is_a_fool_for_five_minutes/164844.html (accessed February 19,2009).

2. Isador Isaac Rabi, quoted in "Great Minds Start With Questions," *Parents Magazine* (September 1993).

3. Danish proverb, http://www.c2i.ntu.edu.sg/AI+CI/Humor/ tlquotes_H.html (accessed February 19, 2009).

4. William H. Danforth, http://www.allthingswilliam.com/creativity. html (accessed February 19, 2009).

Chapter 19: Are You Filling People Up or Sucking Them Dry?

1. John Lubbock, http://thinkexist.com/quotation/to_do_something-however_small-to_make_others/182286.html (accessed February 20, 2009).

2. Edward Spencer, quoted by Warren W. Wiersbe in *The Wiersbe Bible Commentary: New Testament* (Colorado Springs, CO: David C. Cook, 2007), 667.

3. Bruce Larson, http://74.125.95.132/ search?q=cache:N2OuRfnnthUJ:www.akronfpc.org/RC-S080608.pdf+Br uce+Larson,+Wind+%26+Fire,+sand+hill+cranes&hl=en&ct=clnk&cd=2 &gl=us (accessed February 20, 2009).

4. Virginia Arcastle, http://www.giftedleaders.com/quotes.htm (accessed February 20, 2009).

5. Dale Carnegie, *How to Win Friends & Influencee People* (New York, NY: Simon and Schuster, 1981), 227.

6. *Homemade*, March 1992, Source unknown.

7. Donald Laird, quoted in John C. Maxwell, *There's No Such Thing as "Business" Ethics* (Warner Faith, 2003), 41.

8. Richard Nixon, *In the Arena,* http://robbiehilton.com/2008/03/18/ whats-my-motivation/ (accessed February 20, 2009).

9. Henry Ward Beecher, htttp://www.changeyourstars8.com/quotes. html (accessed February 20, 2009).

10. Benjamin West, http://thinkexist.com/quotation/a-kiss-from-my-mother-made-me-a-painter/369301.html (February 20, 2009).

11. George Bernard Shaw, http://www.brainyquote.com/quotes/quotes/g/georgebern109537.html (accessed February 20, 2009).

Chapter 20: If You Ain't the Lead Horse, Watch Your Step

1. John F. Kennedy, http://www.whatquote.com/quotes/John-F--Kennedy/22561-Once-you-say-you-re-.htm (accessed February 20, 2009).

2. Helen Keller, quoted by John C. Maxwell, *Be All You Can Be* (Colorado Springs, CO: David C. Cook, 2007), 51.

3. Phillips Brooks, quoted by John C. Maxwell, *Be All You Can Be* (Colorado Springs, CO: David C. Cook, 2007), 32.

4. Frederic Flach, *Choices,* quoted by John C. Maxwell, *The 17 Essential Qualities of a Team Player* (T. Nelson, 2002), 24.

5. John F. Kennedy, Address to the UN General Assembly, (25 September 1961), http://en.wikiquote.org/wiki/John_F._Kennedy (accessed April 15, 2009).

SECTION SIX: ENCOURAGEMENT

Chapter 21: Offer a Shoulder to Lean On

1. Richard M. DeVos, quoted by Hal Urban, *Positive Words, Powerful Results* (New York, NY: Simon and Schuster, 2004), 69.

2. *Sports Illustrated*, quoted by Wayne Rice and Anthony Campolo, *Hot Illustrations for Youth Talks* (Grand Rapids, MI: Zondervan, 1993), 93.

3. Orison Swett Marden, *Bits & Pieces*, Vol. F/ No. 41, p. 14.

4. Bette Midler, http://thinkexist.com/quotation/the_worst_part_of_success_is_trying_to_find/199447.html (accessed February 20, 2009).

Chapter 22: How Good Can People Be?

1. Les Giblin, quoted by John C. Maxwell, *The 360-Degree Leader Workbook* (Nashville, TN: Thomas Nelson, Inc., 2006), 124.

2. Bob Boyles and Paul Guido, *50 Years of College Football* (Skyhorse Publishing, 2007), 101.

3. Mark Twain, http://www.quotedb.com/quotes/138 (accessed February 20, 2009).

Chapter 23: Reducing the Sting of Criticism

1. David Brinkley, quoted by Karl Iglesias, *The 101 Habits of Highly Successful Screenwriters* (Avon, MA: Adams Media, 2001), 215.

2. Charles Spurgeon, quoted by Sharon Anthony Bower and Gordon Bower, *Asserting Yourself* (Cambridge, MA: Da Capo Press, 1991), 189.

3. O.A. Bautista, Source unknown.

4. Epictetus, Source unknown.

5. Cavett Robert, Source unknown.

6. Abraham Lincoln, quoted by Dale Carnegie, *How to Enjoy Life and Your Job* (New York, NY: Simon and Schuster), 62.

7. George Washington Goethals, Source unknown.

8. Corrie ten Boom, quoted by P.M. Forni, *Choosing Civility* (New York, NY: St. Martin's Press, 2002), 141.

9. Marshall Field, quoted by John Tschohi, *E-Service* (Minneapolis, MN: Best Sellers Publishing), 177.

10. Dilbert's Words of Wisdom, http://www.goodquotes.com/taglines.htm (accessed February 20, 2009).

Chapter 24: Helping People Believe in Themselves

1. John H. Spalding, quoted by Kurt W. Mortensen, *Maximum Influence* (New York, NY: American Management Association, 2004), 119,

2. Yogi Berra, Source unknown.

3. Thomas Edison, Source unknown.

4. *Stand and Deliver*, starring Edward James Olmos, 11 March 1988 (USA).

5. George Bernard Shaw quote, http://thinkexist.com/quotation/the_only_man_who_behaves_sensibly_is_my_tailor-he/188548.html (accessed February 20, 2009).

Section Seven: Understanding

Chapter 25: Whose Language Are You Speaking?

1. Carl Rogers, quoted by India Podsen and Vicki M. Denmark, *Coaching and Mentoring First-year and Student Teachers*, (Larchmont, NY: Eye On Education, Inc., 2000), 133.

2. Robert H. Schuller, *Reach Out for New Life* (Garden Grove, CA: The Cathedral Press, 1991), 150–152.

3. Robert H. Schuller, Source unknown.

4. John Luther, quoted by Sam Deep and Lyle Sussman, *Smart Moves for People in Charge* (Cambridge, MA: Basic Books, 1995), 227.

5. Mark Twain, http://thinkexist.com/quotation/one_learns_through_ the_heart-not_the_eyes_or_the/178119.html (accessed February 20, 2009).

Chapter 26: The Reasons People Do Things

1. Mark Twain, http://www.quotationspage.com/quote/354.html (accessed February 20, 2009).

2. Dale Carnegie, *How to Win Friends and Influence People* (New York, NY: Simon & Schuster, 1981), 33.

3. Bob Conklin, quoted by John C Maxwell, *Be a People Person* (Colorado Springs, CO: David C. Cook, 2007), 90.

4. Lord Chesterfield, Philip Dormer Stanhope Chesterfield, *Selection from the Letters of Lord Chesterfield to His Son and His Godson* (New York, NY: Thomas Y. Crowell & Co., 1904), 176.

5. Anthony Robbins, http://quotationsbook.com/quote/33854/ (accessed February 20, 2009).

6. http://www.thehumorarchives.com/joke/Dilberts_Words_of_ Wisdom (accessed February 20, 2009).

Chapter 27: Putting Yourself in Their World

1. David Augsburger, Source unknown.

2. http://famouspoetsandpoems.com/poets/shel_silverstein/ poems/14823 (accessed February 20, 2009).

3. Brian Tracy, Source Unknown.

Chapter 28: Could You Just Listen?

1. Bernard M. Baruch, Source unknown.

2. John Maxwell, Source unknown.

3. Karl Menninger, quoted by Ira D. Glick, Ellen M. Berman, John F. Clarkin, *Marital and Family Therapy* (Arlington, VA: American Psychiatric Publishing, Inc., 2000), 168.

4. Author unknown, quoted by Gweneth Hartrick Doane and Colleen Varcoe, *Family Nursing as Relational Inquiry* (Philadelphia, PA: Lippincott Williams & Wilkins, 2005), 203.

5. Paul Tournier, quoted by Charles R. Swindoll, *Growing Strong in the Seasons of Life* (Grand Rapids, MI: Zondervan Publishing House, 1983), 69.

6. Source unknown.

7. Unofficial listening study, quoted by John C. Maxwell, *Leadership Gold* (Nashville, TN: Thomas Nelson, Inc., 2008), 50.

8. Mortimer Adler, quoted by Matt Copeland, *Socratic Circles* (Portland, ME: Stenhouse Publishers, 2005), 16–17.

SECTION EIGHT: COMMUNICATION

Chapter 29: For Men Only

1. Archie Bunker, quoted by Paul W. Swets, *The Art of Talking So that People Will Listen* (New York, NY: Simon and Schuster, 1983), 45.

2. Paul Faulkner, *Making Things Right When Things Go Wrong* (PBF Publishing Co, 2006).

3. Helen Rowland, Source unknown.

Chapter 30: Mastering a Rare Secret to Success

1. Lyndon D. Johnson, http://www.infoplease.com/spot/presquotes1.html#wash (accessed February 20, 2009).

2. Henry Ford, quoted by Dale Carnegie, Dorothy Carnegie, Donna Dale Carnegie, *How to Win Friends & Influence People*, (New York NY: Simon & Schuster, 1981), 35.

3. Source unknown.

4. Dick Cavett, http://www.brainyquote.com/quotes/keywords/rare.html (accessed February 20, 2009).

5. Carl Rogers, Source unknown.

6. Abraham Lincoln, quoted by Stephen Denning, *The Secret Language of Leadership* (San Francisco, CA: John Wiley & Sons, Inc., 2007), 42.

7. Ann Landers, Source unknown.

8. Jedd Medefind and Erik Lokkesmoe, *The Revolutionary Communicator* (Lake Mary, FL: Relevant Media Group, 2004), 8–9.

8. George and Nikki Kochler, Source unknown.

9. Malcolm Forbes, Source unknown.

Chapter 31: Untangle Your Horns

1. Carol Tavris, Source unknown.

2. 1984 Orioles vs. Boston, Boston Fire Historical Society and Paul A. Christian, *Boston's Fire Trail*, (Charleston, SC: The History Press, 2007), 114.

3. Sam Markewich, quoted by Ichak Adizes, *Management/ Mismanagement Styles* (Santa Barbara, CA: The Adizes Institute Publishing, 2004), 120.

4. Aristotle, quoted by B.G. Dale, James J. Plunkett, *Quality Costing* (Hampshire, England: Chapman & Hall, 1999), 49.

5. Cullen Hightower, quoted by Gurdeep S. Hura and Mukesh Singhai, *Data and Computer Communications* (Boca Raton, FL: CRC Press LLC, 2001), 659.

6. Matthew 5:25 (KJV).

7. Indira Gandhi, *Christian Science Monitor* (May 17, 1982).

8. *Pulpit Helps* (Chattanooga, TN, 2009).

9. W.C. Fields, http://thinkexist.com/quotation/there_comes_a_time_ in_the_affairs_of_man_when_he/226512.html (accessed February 20, 2009).

Chapter 32: Work Through It

1. W. Grant, http://thinkexist.com/quotation/marriage_is_a_mutual_ admiration_society_where_one/227501.html (accessed February 21, 2009).

2. Andre Maurios, quoted by Carlo D'Este, *Patton* (New York, NY: HarperCollins, 1995), 119.

3. George Levinger, http://www.worldofquotes.com/author/George-Levinger/1/index.html (accessed February 21, 2009).

4. Charles R. Swindoll, *Strike the Original Match* (Grand Rapids, MI: Zondervan Publishing House, 1993), 189.

5. Ogden Nash, http://famouspoetsandpoems.com/poets/ogden_nash/ quotes (accessed February 21, 2009).

6. George Burns, http://www.allgreatquotes.com/funny_quotes331. shtml (accessed February 21, 2009).

Section Nine: Gratitude

Chapter 33: Keep Those Fires Burning

1. Ralph L. Byron, Source unknown.

2. James Dobson, Source unknown.

3. James Smith, quoted by John R. Buri, *How to Love Your Wife* (Tate Publishing LLC, 2006), 80.

4. James Wharton, http://www.slideshare.net/techlistener/marriage (accessed February 21, 2009).

Chapter 34: How to Phrase It When You Want to Praise It

1. Jerry D. Twentier, Source unknown.

2. Jack Benny, http://www.quotationspage.com/quote/311.html (accessed February 21, 2009).

3. Samuel Goldwyn, http://www.quotationspage.com/quote/2814.html (accessed February 21, 2009).

4. Mary Kay Ash, Source unknown.

Chapter 35: Happiness Is Living Every Moment

1. Lucy Swindoll, http://mental-health.families.com/blog/inspirational-quotes-from-inspirational-people (accessed February 21, 2009).

2. Dennis Wholey, quoted by David C. Cook, *The KJV International Bible Lesson Commentary* (Colorado Springs, CO: David C. Cook, 2008), 69.

3. Thomas Szasz, http://www.xquotes.net/219160/Happiness_is_an_imaginary_condition_formerly_often_attribut.html (accessed February 21, 2009).

4. Shirley Temple Black, http://74.125.95.132/search?q=cache:ckmkuFt_nU4J:www.shirleytemplefans.com/report%2520temple%25208.doc+Shirley+Temple+Black%27s+mother-in-law&hl=en&ct=clnk&cd=2&gl=us (accessed February 8, 2009).

5. Norman Cousins, Source unknown.

6. Hugh Downs, http://www.quoteworld.org/quotes/3851 (accessed February 21, 2009).

7. Norman Vincent Peale, Source unknown.

8. Bertrand Russell, http://www.quotationspage.com/quote/27502.html (accessed February 21, 2009).

9. 1980s Harvard study, Source unknown.

10. Dr. Benjamine Spock, http://thinkexist.com/quotation/happiness_is_mostly_a_by-product_of_doing_what/172307.html

11. Helen Keller, http://www.quotationspage.com/quote/1964.html (accessed February 21, 2009).

12. Harold Kushner, *When All You've Ever Wanted Isn't Enough* (New York, NY: Simon & Schuster, 1986), 23.

13. Denis Waitley, http://thinkexist.com/quotation/happiness_cannot_be_traveled_to-owned-earned-worn/296673.html (accessed February 21, 2009).

14. Lou Holtz, quoted by Julia Vitulio-Martin and J. Robert Moskin, *The Executive's Book of Quotations* (Oxford University Press, 1994), 305.

Chapter 36: An Eternal Optimist

1. Paul Harvey, http://www.quotelady.com/subjects/optimism.html (accessed February 21, 2009).

2. Lucille Ball, http://www.quoteworld.org/quotes/936 (accessed February 21, 2009).

3. Richard Wirthlin, Source unknown.

4. Marcus Aurelius, http://www.memorable-quotes.com/marcus+aurelius+antoninus,a592.html (accessed February 21, 2009).

5. Source unknown.

6. *Los Angeles Times* Syndicate.

SECTION TEN: GENEROSITY

Chapter 37: A Touch of Kindness

1. Harold S. Kushner, Source unknown.

2. Francis Schaeffer, Source unknown.

3. Ann Landers, http://titan.iwu.edu/~jplath/Quoth.html (accessed February 22, 2009).

Chapter 38: An Act of Compassion

1. George Washington Carver, http://www.quotationspage.com/quote/26308.html (accessed February 22, 2009).

2. Cameron Lee, *Unexpected Blessing* (Downer's Grove, IL: InterVarsity Press, 2004), 170.

3. Lao-tse, http://thinkexist.com/quotation/kindness_in_words_creates_confidence-kindness_in/11355.html (accessed February 22, 2009).

Chapter 39: You Can't Take Back the Words

1. Robert Louis Stevenson, quoted by Chaim Stern, *Day by Day* (Boston, MA: Beacon Press, 2000), 274.

2. Lisa Kirk, http://thinkexist.com/quotation/a_gossip_is_one_who_talks_to_you_about_others-a/191042.html (accessed February 22, 2009).

Chapter 40: The Mystery of Money

1. Jean Kerr, http://thinkexist.com/quotes/with/keyword/poor_person/ (accessed February 22, 2009).

2. George S. Clason, *The Richest Man in Babylon* (New York, NY: Penguin Putnam, 1955).

3. Brian Harbour, *Living Obediently* (Baptist Sunday School Board, 1992).

4. Larry Burkett, http://www.crown.org/library/ViewArticle.aspx?ArticleId=340 (accessed February 22, 2009).

5. *Working Well,* Source unknown.

6. James Moffatt, quoted by Adrian furnham and Michael Argyle, *The Psychology of Money* (New York, NY: Routledge, 1998), 153.

7. John M. Templeton, Source unknown.

8. John Wesley, http://www.project1615.org/quotes.htm (accessed February 22, 2009).

9. http://www.geocities.com/campuschristians_sjc/articles/alittlemore.html (accessed February 22, 2009).

10. John Maxwell, Source unknown.

11. E. Stanley Jones, http://eugenecho.wordpress.com/2007/12/06/fight-poverty-a-vision-of-redistribution/ (accessed February 22, 2009).

Section Eleven: EMPATHY

Chapter 41: A Cure for Loneliness.

1. Lily Tomlin, http://en.thinkexist.com/quotes/lily_tomlin/ (accessed February 22, 2009).

2. http://query.nytimes.com/gst/fullpage.html?res=9F0CE7D8103DF93BA15753C1A965958260&sec=&spon= (accessed February 23, 2009).

3. Ralph Waldo Emerson, http://thinkexist.com/quotation/you_cannot_do_a_kindness_too_soon-for_you_never/224574.html (accessed February 23, 2009).

4. Ann Landers, http://www.growingthroughgrief.com/resources_quotes.html (accessed February 23, 2009).

Chapter 42: Make a Difference in People's Lives

1. Horace Mann, http://www.livinglifefully.com/servingothers.htm (accessed February 23, 2009).

2. http://peterjblackburn.com/bstud/bsisaiah07.pdf (accessed February 23, 2009).

3. Rabbi Harold Kushner, Source unknown.

4. Ari Kiev, Source unknown.

Chapter 43: Getting Even

1. Henry Drummond, *Drummond's Addresses* (Chicago, IL: W. B. Conkey, Co., 1900), 36.

2. Quoted by Zig Ziglar, http://www.geocities.com/tangental/xquotes.htm (accessed February 23, 2009).

3. James M. Barrie, http://www.brainyquote.com/quotes/authors/j/james_m_barrie.html (accessed February 23, 2009).

Chapter 44: Never Assume You're Pedaling Together

1. Marcus Aurelius, http://www.innersports.org/MarcusAurelius.htm (accessed February 23 2009).

2. Gerhard Gschwandtner, http://thinkexist.com/quotes/with/keyword/common_cause/ (accessed February 23, 2009).

Section Twelve: Hope

Chapter 45: You Can Make a Difference

1.Harvey Mackay, *Pushing the Envelope: How to Do it All the Way to the Top* (New York, NY; Ballantine, 1999), 247.

2. Clare Booth Luce, *Life* magazine (August 7, 1964).

3. Mother Theresa, http://thinkexist.com/quotation/loneliness_and_the_feeling_of_being_unwanted_is/149759.html (accessed February 23, 2009).

Chapter 46: How Do People Feel Around You?

1. Irwin Federman, http://www.1-love-quotes.com/20186.htm (accessed February 23, 2009).

2. Cavett Robert, http://www.bettersermons.org/article.php?id=288 (accessed February 23, 2009).

Chapter 47: Give Yourself Away

1. Anthony Robbins, http://thinkexist.com/quotation/only_those_ who_have_learned_the_power_of_sincere/322114.html (accessed February 23, 2009).

2. Eric Butterworth, Source unknown.

3. Robert Louis Stevenson, http://thinkexist.com/quotation/don-t_ judge_each_day_by_the_harvest_you_reap_but/223119.html (accessed February 23, 2009).

4. https://www.discoveryseries.org/devotionals/our-daily-bread/1996/07/15/devotion.aspx (accessed February 23, 2009).

5. Eleanor Roosevelt, *You Learn by Living* (Louisville, KY: Westminster John Knox Press, 1960), 95.

6. Elvis Presley, http://www.inc.com/magazine/19930901/3705.html (accessed Febrary 23, 2009).

7. General William Booth, Source unknown.

8. John D. Rockefelle, Sr., Source unknown.

9. Robert Fulghum, *All I Really Need to Know I Learned in Kindergarten* (New York, NY: The Ballantine Publishing Group, 1988), 117.

10. John Wesley, http://thinkexist.com/quotation/do_all_the_good_ you_can-in_all_the_ways_you_can/174178.html (accessed February 23, 2009).

11. Henry Ford, Sr., http://www.appleseeds.org/Oct_99.htm (accessed February 23, 2009).

12. Karl Menninger, quoted by Mary Jane Ryan, *The Happiness Makeover*, (Random House, Inc., 2005), 137.

Chapter 48: One Thing at a Time

1. Franklin Field, http://www.discover-time-management.com/time-management-quotes.html (accessed February 23, 2009).

2. Larry King, http://thinkexist.com/quotes/with/keyword/ effectively/4.html (accessed February 23, 2009).

About the Author

G LENN VAN EKEREN IS THE Executive Vice President for Vetter Health Services in Omaha, Nebraska—a company committed to providing "dignity in life" for the elderly. For the past thirty years, Glenn's primary profession has been helping people grow. His passion as a leader is to create a work environment where people feel good about themselves, their jobs, the people they work with, the people they serve, and their organizations.

As a professional speaker, he is known for his inspiring, enthusiastic, and down-to-earth approach for maximizing people and organizational potential. Glenn has also traveled the country providing more than one thousand seminars and keynote addresses to nearly one hundred thousand people. Glenn's motto in life is "to live every moment of every day to the fullest." His seminars and books will make you laugh, think, feel great, look at life in a fresh way, and be inspired to stretch toward your potential. His messages capture people's attention, stir emotions, and provide practical strategies for personal and organizational growth.

Since 1988, Glenn has authored several books, including the original *Speaker's Sourcebook* and the best-selling *Speaker's Sourcebook II, 12 Simple Secrets of Happiness: Finding Joy in Everyday Relationships, 12 Simple Secrets of Happiness at Work: Finding*

Fulfillment, Reaping Rewards, and *12 Simple Secrets of Happiness in a Topsy-Turvy World.* He is a featured author in several *Chicken Soup for the Soul* books, as well as the editor of *Braude's Treasury of Wit & Humor for All Occasions,* and *The Complete Speaker's & Toastmaster's Library.* Glenn has penned numerous articles for various professional publications.